26 quick

Stitched Elements

ENDLESS JEWELRY POSSIBILITIES

Thomasin Alyxander

Kalmbach Books

Waukesha, WI

Dedicated to Rhea Lozier, Mabel Lozier, Iris Kelton, and all of your crafty mothers and grandmothers.

Kalmbach Books
21027 Crossroads Circle
Waukesha, Wisconsin 53186
www.JewelryAndBeadingStore.com

Lettered step-by-step photos by Nedda Rovelli. Illustrations by the author. All other photography © 2015 Kalmbach Books except where otherwise noted.

Published in 2015
19 18 17 16 15   1 2 3 4 5

Manufactured in the United States of America

ISBN: 978-1-62700-203-5
EISBN: 978-1-62700-204-2

Editor: Erica Swanson
Book Design: Lisa Bergman
Photographers: William Zubach, James Forbes

Library of Congress Control Number: 2015930761

Contents

Foreword

What is happening to seed beading? This beloved art form, steeped in tradition, is evolving at an extraordinary pace. With the increased variety of shaped beads appearing throughout bead stores and the rise of two-hole beading as an art form, there are more color, texture, and dimensional possibilities than ever. The basic fundamentals of beading have not changed, but beaders have been adapting their skills to embrace current design innovations. As a manufacturer, jewelry designer, and creator of pressed glass beads, including the *CzechMates™* two-hole beading system, I understand how overwhelming it can be to jump from one new design concept to the next. In order to help beaders learn how to work with my new beads, I assembled a team of leading artists (the *Starman TrendSetters*) to explore new stitch paths and design concepts that the new shapes make possible. I invited Alyx to be a part of the team because of her natural ability to make dimensional designs that resonate with beaders everywhere. Alyx is an experienced, visionary designer with an innate teaching ability that makes this book an essential guide for those who are transitioning into modern beading.

With the vast amount of shaped beads available to seed beaders today, now is a good time to reflect on how far design techniques have evolved to accommodate them. The advancements have come about, not by chance, but by the efforts of innovative artists like Alyx. Her distinctive beading style first caught my attention three years ago with her unconventional usage of CzechMates Tile beads in her designs. Two-hole beading was an emerging concept, and I knew that her dimensional skills would make her a good fit for TrendSetters. I challenged the team to use the new bead shape prototypes I was developing, the Brick and the Lentil. Not only did she pioneer new independent stitch methods, but she also combined multiple concepts together into wearable works of art.

It's not easy to jump into the new world of beading without direction, but I am confident that Alyx's artistic vision will provide guidance and inspire beaders to develop their own beading style. She is not only gifted with the ability to make inventing new techniques look easy, but her talent also lies with her ability to present simplified, easy-to-follow instructions. Her method-based, component approach to jewelry making breaks down each new learned concept into a fundamental skill that can be expanded upon in future designs.

The emergence of new beads and modern beading techniques has given seed beaders the opportunity to create designs that transcend traditional beadwork. It excites me to create beads with the support of ground-breaking artists, like Alyx, inventing complementary new stitch techniques. I admire her passion to educate and inspire beaders to try something new. It is her passion for the craft that reaffirms my commitment to the future of this expanding art form.

Nichole Starman
Director, Starman, Inc.

Introduction

The inspiration for this book arose from several different encounters I had in classes I was teaching. Sometimes a student would only make one of something to wear as a pendant when I had intended the project to be a pair of earrings. Once, a little beadwoven wreath I had intended to be a Christmas tree ornament turned out to be a fabulous pair of earrings. Another time, a student came back for help with earrings because she'd lost the instructions, and it turned out that the project was actually a bracelet. Another student stretched me by asking if a bracelet could be made into earrings or made double-wide. Their questions made me realize that presenting a design as a project limits the design's potential. *The idea to create elements was born.*

Elements are only the start—each project uses or develops at least one element into a piece of jewelry. Some of the projects are simple earrings and bracelets, which are perfect for when you want a shorter piece or something repetitive or less daunting. Other bracelets and necklaces are handy when you're ready to sink your teeth into a project and produce a piece of wearable art. Even though this is a beadweaving book, some projects include some basic wirework or stringing techniques. Combining these techniques with beadweaving skills will open new horizons for your jewelry-making. (If you're unsure of any techniques, please flip to the Basics section for easy reference.)

My hope is that this book will let your inner designer out to play. After all, we beaders make our jewelry because we love the satisfaction that comes with the process of creation. For us, the word "fashion" is a mere collection of syllables. We'll make what we like in the colors we like; we don't care what the Devil in Prada thinks this season's palette is. After you've gotten the feel for how the components work together by completing some of the projects, use the components as building blocks for your own designs—this book represents only a drop in the ocean of possibilities. There are lots of ideas waiting for someone to find them in this book! I know, for I found it difficult to stop writing it because I kept thinking of things to add and more things to do with what was already there.

Cheers!
Thomasin Alyxander

elements

From the intense eye through the tips of the dagger rays, this component bursts with the colors of suns from imaginary worlds! Mesmerizing and dramatic, the sunburst is a gorgeous feature in any design. The process for making the 9-point Sunburst is the same as for making the 8-point. Follow the repetitions or counts given in brackets to make the 9-point version.

materials per element
8-point link
- 12mm rivoli
- 8 two-hole daggers
- 8 11º seed beads
- .5g 15º seed beads, color F
- .25g 15ºs, color G
- Size D nylon thread

9-point link
- 14mm rivoli or button bead
- 9 two-hole daggers
- 9 11ºs
- .5g 15ºs, color F
- .5g 15ºs, color G
- Size D nylon thread

tools
- Size 12 and 13 needles
- Chainnose pliers
- Thread conditioner
- Thread snips

1. Stretch and condition 2 yd. thread. Thread a needle on one end.

2. Pick up a dagger and an 11º seed bead eight [nine] times. Sew through the hole close to the tip of the dagger. Sew back through the first dagger and 11º, leaving a 12" tail **(photo a)**.

3. Pick up three color F 15º seed beads. Sew through the free hole in the closest dagger **(fig. 1)**.

4. Pick up three Fs. Sew through an 11º, and pass back through two Fs **(fig. 2)**.

5. Pick up an F. Sew through the free hole in the dagger **(fig. 3)**.

6. Repeat steps 4 and 5 six [seven] times. Pick up an F. Sew through two Fs and an 11º. Enter the 11º on the side that is next to the dagger you just sewed through **(photo b, fig. 4)**.

7. Pick up two color G 15ºs, an F, and two more Gs. Sew through an 11º, a dagger, and the next 11º. The beads you picked up will form a circle **(fig. 5)**.

8. Repeat step 7 seven [eight] more times. Continue through two Gs and an F.

9. Pick up two Gs, an F, and two Gs. Sew through the F in the next loop **(fig. 6)**. Repeat seven [eight] times. Continue through two Gs and an F. Set this needle aside.

10. Thread a needle on the tail. Weave the thread in through the dagger-11º thread path, securing the thread with a couple of slip knots. Trim the excess thread from the tail only.

11. Return to the needle you set aside. Pick up two Fs. Skip an F, and sew through the next F **(fig. 7)**. Repeat seven [eight] times. When you're about halfway around, place the rivoli in the netting face-up.

12. Rivoli only: Sew through just the Fs picked up in step 11. Keep your tension tight so that the Fs get drawn into the center.
Button bead only: Pick up a G and sew through two Fs. Repeat seven [eight] times.

13. After you have finished, sew around the center and out through one of the point Fs **(photo c)**.

14. Pick up three Fs. Sew through an F, a dagger, and a second F **(fig. 8, a–b)**.

15. Pick up three Fs. Sew through the nearest point F, and sew back through the three Fs **(c–e)**. Continue through an F, a dagger, and a second F **(f–g)**. Repeat six [seven] more times.

16. After you pass through the last F, dagger, and F, continue up through three Fs and through the point F **(fig. 9, a–b)**. Sew back down through three Fs and continue through an F and a dagger **(c–d)**. Bundle up the remaining thread (Basics). This will protect the thread until you are ready to refer to the Sunburst Swag (p. 43) or the Herringbone Bar Connector (p. 45).

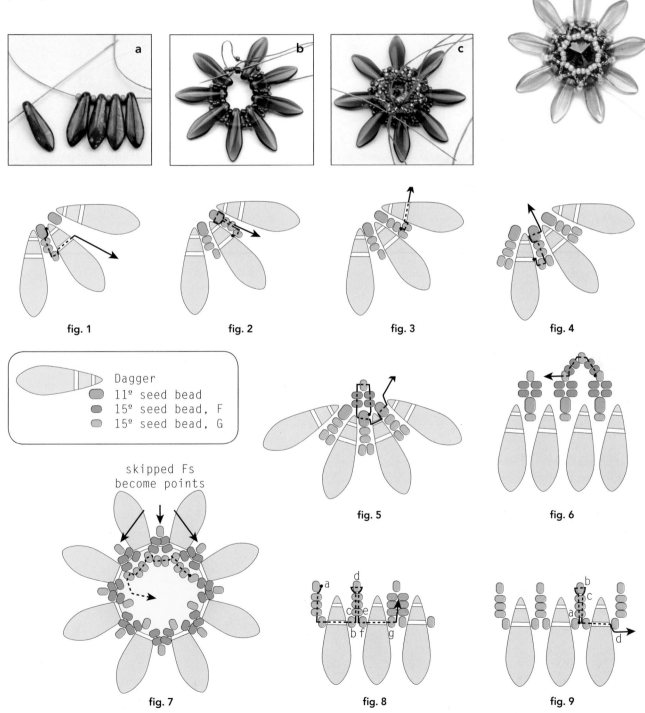

Dagger
11º seed bead
15º seed bead, F
15º seed bead, G

fig. 1

fig. 2

fig. 3

fig. 4

skipped Fs become points

fig. 5

fig. 6

fig. 7

fig. 8

fig. 9

Beautifully textured, these rings are surprisingly light and lacy without being fragile. They are very versatile; you can make earrings with them, use them as links, or even use one as a Y-connector at the front of a necklace.

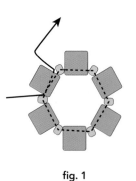
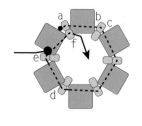

materials per element
- **6** tile beads
- **6** 4mm bicone crystals
- **12** 3mm crystal pearls
- **.75g** 11º seed beads
- **.75g** 15º seed beads
- Size D nylon thread

other materials
- 4mm soldered jump rings as required by your project

tools
- Size 10 and 12 needles
- Silicon thread conditioner
- Thread snips

1. Stretch and condition 2 yd. thread, and thread a size 12 needle. Pick up a tile bead and an 11º seed bead six times. Slide the beads to 8" from the tail end, and sew back through the first tile so the beads form a ring **(fig. 1)**.

2. Sew through the same holes in the tiles that you already used in step 1: Pick up an 11º, and sew through the next tile **(fig. 2, a–b)**. Repeat four times **(c–d)**. Pick up an 11º, and tie the threads together, pulling the beads into a ring. Sew through a tile and an 11º **(e–f)**.

3. Pick up a 15º seed bead, an 11º, a pearl, an 11º, and a 15º. Sew through one of the next two 11ºs **(fig. 3)**. Repeat five more times, keeping the pearl swags on the same side. After the last swag, continue through a tile

and an 11º that does NOT have a swag **(photo a)**. Sew pearl swags onto the back of the medallion, sewing through the free 11ºs. After the twelfth swag, continue through a 15º, an 11º, and a pearl **(fig. 4)**.

4. Set the working needle aside. Thread a needle on the tail, and weave to the center of the ring. Secure the thread with a couple of slip knots. Hide the knots inside the tiles, and trim the excess tail thread.

5. Pick up four 15ºs and an 11º. Sew through the free hole in the tile **(fig. 5, a–b)**. Pick up an 11º and four 15ºs. Sew through a pearl, an 11º, a 15º, an 11º, a 15º, an 11º, and a pearl **(c–d)**. Repeat five times until you reach the pearl where you started. Sew through an 11º, a 15º, an 11º, a tile, and an 11º. Sew through the 11º on the

▢	Tile
◇	Bicone
○	Pearl
▭	11º seed bead
●	15º seed bead

fig. 1   fig. 2   fig. 3

side without the seed bead swags **(photo b)**. Continue through a 15º, an 11º, and a pearl.

6. Pick up four 15ºs. Sew through an 11º, a tile, and an 11º **(fig. 6, a–b)**. Pick up four 15ºs, and sew through a pearl, an 11º, a 15º, an 11º, a 15º, an 11º, and a pearl **(c–d)**. Repeat five times. Continue through four 15ºs, an 11º, a tile, and an 11º. Pick up a 4mm bicone crystal, and sew through an 11º, a tile, and an 11º **(fig. 7)**. Repeat five more times, and end by sewing through a bicone. Bundle up your threads (Basics), or continue to step 7 to finish off the link.

7. Pick up four 15ºs and an 11º. Sew through a soldered jump ring **(fig. 8, a–b)**. Sew back through the beads just picked up and the bicone **(c–d)**. Pick up four 15ºs, and sew through the 11º and the jump ring. Sew back through the 11º, the 15ºs you just picked up, and the bicone. Sew through the beads again to reinforce the jump ring. If you need another jump ring, sew through an 11º, a tile, an 11º, and a bicone as needed to get to the right location. For a link, sew until you pass through the bicone directly opposite the first connection **(fig. 9)**. For a Y-connector, place a jump ring on every other bicone **(fig. 10)**.

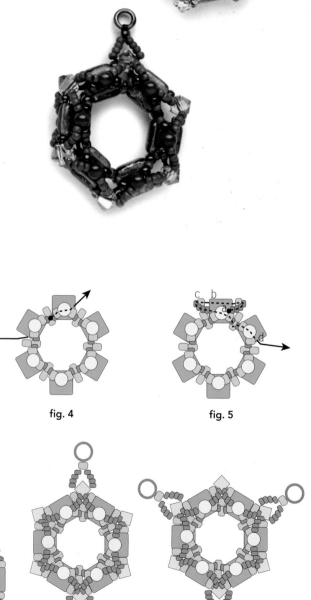

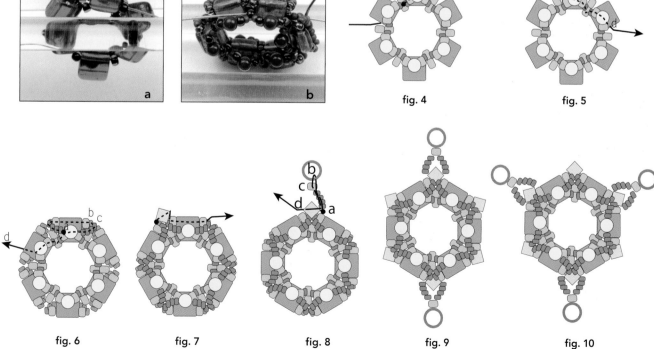

a

b

fig. 4

fig. 5

fig. 6

fig. 7

fig. 8

fig. 9

fig. 10

Because the medallion is beaded on both sides, a pair of them make beautiful earrings—let them swing so that people can fully appreciate your work! The subtle asymmetry gives the impression of movement and adds visual interest when you use the medallion as a link or as a Y-connector.

materials per element
- **6** tile beads
- **6** 4mm crystal bicones
- **18** 3mm crystal pearls
- **.5g** 11º seed beads
- **.5g** 15º seed beads
- Size D nylon thread

other materials
- 4mm soldered jump rings as required for your project

tools
- Size 10 and 12 needles
- Silicon thread conditioner
- Thread snips

1. Stretch and condition approximately 1½ yd. thread. Thread a size 10 or 12 needle (be prepared to step down to a size 12 toward the end if you start with a 10). String a stop bead, leaving an 8" tail.

2. Pick up a tile, an 11º seed bead, four 15º seed beads, an 11º, a tile, an 11º, two 15ºs, and an 11º. Sew through the free hole in the second tile (**fig. 1, a–b**). Pick up a 15º, an 11º, a pearl, an 11º, and a 15º. Sew through the free hole in the first tile, starting on the stop bead side (**c–d**). Pick up an 11º and a 15º, and sew through an 11º, the first hole of the second tile, and an 11º (**e–f**).

3. Pick up four 15ºs, an 11º, a tile, an 11º, two 15ºs, and an 11º. Sew through the free hole in the tile (**fig. 2, a**). Pick up a 15º, an 11º, a pearl, and an 11º. Sew through a 15º, a tile, and an 11º (**b–c**). Pick up a 15º. Sew through an 11º, a tile, and an 11º (**d–e**). Repeat this step three more times. Remove the stop bead. Pick up four 15ºs and an 11º, and sew through a tile and an 11º (**fig. 3, a–b**). Pick up two 15ºs, and sew through an 11º, a tile, and a 15º (**c–d**). Pick up an 11º, a pearl, and an 11º, and sew through a 15º, a tile, and an 11º (**e–f**). Pick up a 15º, and sew through an 11º, a tile, an 11º, and two 15ºs (**g–h**).

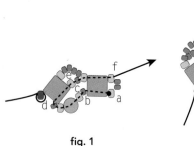

fig. 1

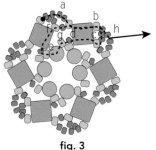

fig. 2

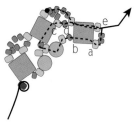

fig. 3

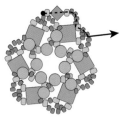

fig. 4

4. Pick up an 11º, a bicone, an 11º, and four 15ºs, and sew through an 11º and two 15ºs (**fig. 4**). Repeat four times. Pick up an 11º, a bicone, an 11º, and four 15ºs, and sew through an 11º, four 15ºs, and an 11º (**photo a**).

5. Pick up a 15º, a pearl, and a 15º, and sew through an 11º and a pearl (**photo b**).

It can be mystifying as to which 11º you are supposed to sew through. Don't sew through the one that is in a straight line with the 15º and tiles. Sew through the 11º that is somewhat below the tile, as shown in photo b.

6. Pick up a 15º, a pearl, and a 15º, and sew through an 11º directly under a bicone (**photo c**). Sew back through the 15º, pearl, and 15º, and sew through an 11º and a pearl. Repeat four times. Sew through a 15º, a pearl, a 15º, and an 11º.

7. Flip the medallion over and repeat steps 5 and 6. This can be confusing, because you are working in the opposite direction as before. Keep in mind that you will sew through the same beads as you did on the first side. When done, work your needle so that it passes through an 11º, a bicone, and an 11º.

8. Weave in the tail as close to the center as you can, securing it with a couple of slip knots. Trim the excess tail thread. If you are not going to finish the component at this time, bundle up the working thread (Basics). Otherwise, pick up five 15ºs and an 11º (**fig. 5, a–b**), and sew through a soldered jump ring and back through an 11º, five 15ºs, an 11º, a bicone, and an 11º (**c–d**).

9. Pick up five 15ºs, and sew through the 11º and the jump ring and back through the five 15ºs you just picked up. Sew through the beads again to strengthen the jump ring connection. To add a second jump ring, sew along the edge to the opposite side of the link and repeat (**fig. 6**). To make a Y-connector, sew a jump ring to every other bicone (**fig. 7**).

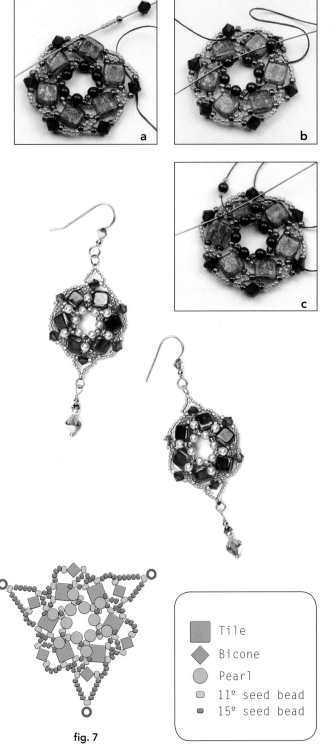

fig. 5   fig. 6   fig. 7

⬛	Tile	
◆	Bicone	
⬭	Pearl	
▫	11º seed bead	
▪	15º seed bead	

Feast your eyes on these beautiful little jewels—they really are eye candy! And like any delicious treat, it's hard to stop at just one.

materials per element
- 14mm square crystal ring or cosmic ring
- **4** two-hole brick beads
- **8** 3mm crystal bicones
- **4** 3mm crystal pearls
- .5g 11º seed beads
- .5g 15º seed beads
- Size D nylon thread

tools
- Size 12 needles
- Silicon thread conditioner
- Thread snips

1. Stretch and condition 5' thread, and thread a needle on one end. String a stop bead and leave an 18" tail. Pick up a brick bead and three 11º seed beads four times, and sew back through the first brick and 11º **(fig. 1)**. Skip the middle 11º and sew through an 11º, a brick, and an 11º **(fig. 2, a–b)**. Repeat three times. Pull the skipped beads to the outside, if necessary. Continue through an 11º and a brick **(c–d)**.

2. Pick up three 15º seed beads. Sew through the free hole in the brick **(fig. 3, a–b)**. Pick up three 15ºs, and sew through the brick, two 11ºs, and a brick **(c–d)**. Repeat this step three times. Sew through three 15ºs **(e)**.

3. Pick up two 15ºs, an 11º, two 15ºs, two 11ºs, two 15ºs, an 11º, and two 15ºs, and sew through three 15ºs, the middle 11º, and three 15ºs **(fig. 4, a–b)**. Start with the

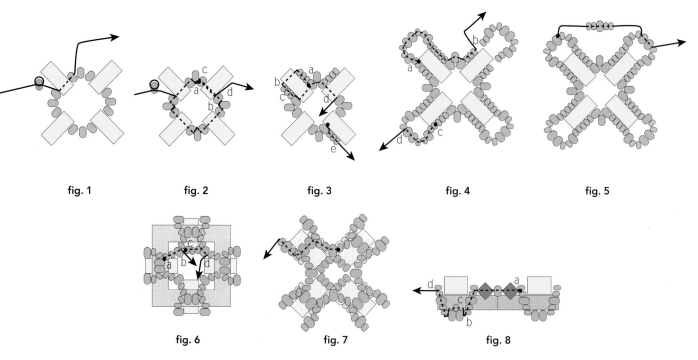

fig. 1   fig. 2   fig. 3   fig. 4   fig. 5

fig. 6   fig. 7   fig. 8

three 15ºs on the other side of the brick where your thread is. Repeat three times. Continue through two 15ºs, an 11º, two 15ºs, and two 11ºs **(c–d)**.

4. Hold the crystal ring face down on the bricks. The points of the square ring go between the bricks. Pick up two 15ºs, an 11º, and two 15ºs, and sew through the center two 11ºs on the next seed bead loop **(fig. 5)**. Repeat three times. Continue through the first two 15ºs and 11º you picked up in this step **(fig. 6, a–b)**.

5. Pick up three 15ºs and sew through an 11º **(c–d)**. Repeat three times. Sew through just the 15ºs to tighten your tension and pull them slightly into the center. Sew through an 11º, two 15ºs, two 11ºs, two 15ºs, an 11º, and a 15º **(fig. 7)**.

6. Pick up a bicone, an 11º and a bicone, and sew through a 15º, an 11º, and two 15ºs **(fig. 8, a–b)**. Pick up a 15º, and sew through two 15ºs, an 11º, and a 15º **(c–d)**. Repeat this step three times. Sew through all the beads in this step again. End by sewing through a crystal, an 11º, and a crystal. If you are going to string the Turban, weave only the working thread in along this same thread path, securing it with a couple of slip knots. Otherwise, remove the needle and bundle your thread (Basics). Remove the stop bead. Thread a

needle on the tail and sew through two 11ºs. (The second 11º is one of the skipped ones.)

7. Pick up two 15ºs, a pearl, and two 15ºs. Sew through the next skipped 11º **(fig. 9, a–b)**. Repeat this step three times, and continue through two 15ºs and a pearl **(c–d)**. Pick up an 11º, and sew through a pearl **(fig. 10)**. Repeat three times. Sew through the pearls and 11ºs again to tighten your tension.

If you feel the center lacks definition, weave through just the pearls and 15ºs again.

8. If you are going to string the Turban, secure the thread in the center ring of pearls and 11ºs with a couple of slip knots. Otherwise, remove the needle and bundle your thread.

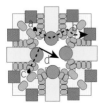

fig. 9

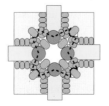

fig. 10

	Brick
◆	3mm bicone
●	3mm crystal pearl
●	11º seed bead
●	15º seed bead

15

Impressive yet dainty, this component adds gravitas to any design that includes it. It can be a focal pendant, an accent drop, or even a bar in a two-strand bracelet. As a bonus, it's surprisingly fast and easy to make.

materials per element
- **14mm** crystal square ring
- **4** brick beads
- **4** 3mm crystal pearls, color A
- **4** 3mm crystal pearls, color B
- **.5g** 11º seed beads
- **.5g** 15º seed beads
- Size D nylon thread

tools
- Size 12 needles
- Silicon thread conditioner
- Thread snips
- Pencil with eraser

1. Stretch and condition 5' thread, and thread a needle on one end. String on a stop bead and leave an 18" tail. Pick up twenty 11ºs, and sew back through the first four 11ºs to form a ring **(fig. 1)**.

2. Skip an 11º. Sew through four 11ºs. Repeat this step three times. Continue through the first skipped 11º **(fig. 2)**. *Pick up a 15º, two 11ºs, a 15º, a brick, a 15º, two 11ºs, and a 15º, and sew through the next skipped 11º **(fig. 3, a–b)**. Repeat from the * three times. Continue through a 15º, two 11ºs, a 15º, and a brick **(c–d)**.

3. Pick up three 15ºs. Sew through the free hole in the brick **(fig. 4, a–b)**. Pick up three 15ºs. Sew through the other hole in the brick, a 15º, two 11ºs, a 15º, an 11º, a 15º, two 11ºs, a 15º, and a brick **(c–d)**. Repeat this step three times. Continue through three 15ºs.

4. Pick up two 15ºs, an 11º, a color A pearl, an 11º, and two 15ºs, and sew through three 15ºs on the next brick, heading into the center **(fig. 5, a–b)**. Pick up two 15ºs, two 11ºs, and two 15ºs, and sew through three 15ºs on the same brick, heading away from the center **(c–d)**. Repeat this step three times. Keep the seed bead loop crossing on the same sides of the bricks. Continue through two 15ºs, an 11º, a pearl, and an 11º.

5. Place the crystal square inside the beadwork. The points go between bricks. Pick up a color B pearl, and sew through an 11º, an A, and an 11º **(fig. 6, a–b)**. Repeat three times. Continue through a B. *Pick up four

16

15ºs, and sew through the next B (c–d). Repeat from the * three times. Continue through four 15ºs. **Pick up two 15ºs. Sew through the next four 15ºs (e–f). Repeat from the ** three times. Continue through two 15ºs. Sew through just the center 15ºs again.

6. If you are going to string the component, secure the working thread in the circle with the pearls and 11ºs. Remove the stop bead and secure the tail in the 11ºs in the original ring. Trim the excess thread. Push the 15ºs in the center of the crystal down with a pencil eraser (**photo**). Otherwise, bundle your threads (Basics). Once the threads are woven in, press down the 15ºs in the center.

A single Temple makes an elegant pendant.

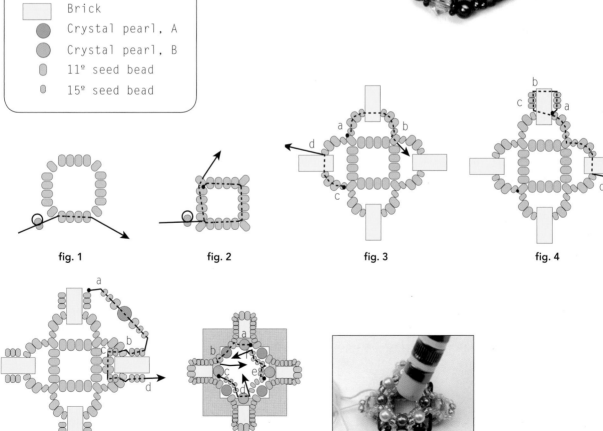

	Brick
●	Crystal pearl, A
●	Crystal pearl, B
◗	11º seed bead
▪	15º seed bead

fig. 1

fig. 2

fig. 3

fig. 4

fig. 5

fig. 6

The way the seed beads float above the negative space in the crystal brings to mind the seats of those old-fashioned caned chairs. Technically a bezel, this component is a striking way to frame a square crystal ring.

materials per element
- 14mm square ring
- 4 glass bricks
- 8 3mm crystal pearls
- .75g 11º seed beads
- .5g 15º seed beads
- Size D nylon thread

tools
- Size 12 needles
- Silicon thread conditioner
- Thread snips

1. Stretch and condition 5' thread, and thread a needle on one end. Attach a stop bead 2' from the tail. Pick up two 11ºs and seven 15ºs four times. Sew back through the first two 11ºs so the beads form a ring. *Pick up a brick and three 15ºs. Sew through the free hole in the brick **(fig. 1, a–b)**. Sew through the two 11ºs so the brick sits on top of them, then sew through seven 15ºs and two 11ºs **(c–d)**. Repeat from the * three times. Continue through a brick and three 15ºs.

2. Pick up a 15º, an 11º, a pearl, a 15º, two 11ºs, a 15º, a pearl, an 11º and a 15º, and sew through the three 15ºs on the next brick **(fig. 2)**. Repeat this step three times, and continue through a 15º, an 11º, a pearl, a 15º, and two 11ºs. Set the crystal square face up in the center. (The points go between the bricks.)

3. Pick up an 11º. Sew through the center two 11ºs on the next loop **(fig. 3, a–b)**. Repeat this step three times. Continue through an 11º between the pairs of 11ºs. *Pick up a 15º, and sew through an 11º you picked up in this step **(c–d)**. Repeat from the * three times. Continue through two 11ºs, a 15º, a pearl, an 11º and five 15ºs. (The five 15ºs are on top of a brick.)

4. Pick up four 15ºs, and sew through three center 15ºs on the back **(fig. 4, a–b)**. Pick up four 15ºs, and sew through the five 15ºs on the next brick. Repeat this step three times. Weave the thread into the top of the element and secure it with a couple of slip knots. Trim the excess thread. If you are going to string the element, remove the stop bead, thread a needle on the tail, and weave into the center ring of beads on the back. Hide the knots in the 15ºs and do not clog up the 11ºs. Otherwise, bundle the tail thread (Basics).

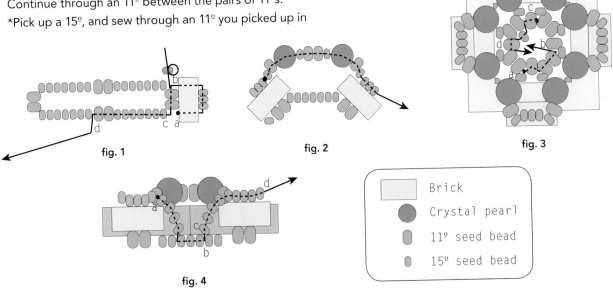

fig. 1

fig. 2

fig. 3

fig. 4

	Brick
	Crystal pearl
	11º seed bead
	15º seed bead

This component adds a dash and a splash of joy to everything. The finished almond shape stands out from other components and livens up the overall look of your finished design.

materials per element
- **6** tile beads
- **6** lentils (one hole)
- **12** berry beads
- **.25g** 11º seed beads
- **.1g** 15º seed beads
- Size D nylon thread

other materials
- 4mm soldered jump rings as required by your project

tools
- Size 12 needles
- Stop bead
- Silicon thread conditioner
- Thread snips

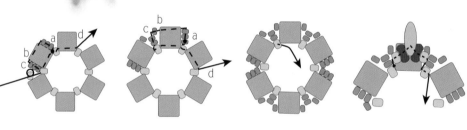

fig. 1	fig. 2	fig. 3	fig. 4

▢	Tile
⬭	Lentil (one hole)
⬗	Berry bead
▫	11º seed bead
●	15º seed bead

1. Stretch and condition 4½' thread, and thread a needle. Attach a stop bead 18" from the tail. Pick up an 11º and a tile six times, and sew back through the first 11º and tile.

2. Pick up three 15ºs, and sew through the free hole in the tile **(fig. 1, a–b)**. Pick up three 15ºs, and sew through the tile, an 11º, and the next tile **(c–d)**.

3. Pick up three 15ºs. Sew through the free hole in the tile **(fig. 2, a–b)**. Pick up a 15º, and sew through two 15ºs, a tile, an 11º, and a tile **(c–d)**. Repeat this step.

4. Repeat steps 2 and 3. Continue through an 11º **(fig. 3)**.

5. Pick up an 11º, a berry bead, a lentil, a berry, and an 11º. Sew through the next 11º between tiles **(fig. 4)**. Repeat five times.

For a variation, you can pick a 15º, an 11º, a berry, a lentil, a berry, an 11º, and a 15º, as shown in many of my samples.

6. Sew through just the beads in the swags from step 5 again, including the 15ºs if you did the variation. Sew through the 11º in the original ring of tiles and the 11º that is opposite the 11º with the tail. Remove the stop bead.

If you are not sure yet how you will use the element, bundle your threads. To attach soldered jump rings, refer to the Festival Earrings, p. 68. To connect elements together, refer to the Festival Bracelet, p. 81.

These petite triangle-shaped beads give texture to a design without adding bulk. This link is an excellent addition to a necklace design if you want to make a set—and Origami earrings or a bracelet will be lovely complements to your design.

materials per element
- **4** two-hole triangles
- **4** 3mm crystal pearls
- **.25g** 11º seed beads
- **.25g** 15º seed beads
- **2** 4mm soldered jump rings
- Size D nylon thread

tools
- Size 10 and 12 needles
- Silicon thread conditioner
- Thread snips

If you plan to connect the origami links, subsequent origami links will only need three crystal pearls.

1. Stretch and condition 1 yd. thread, and thread on a size 10 needle.

2. Pick up a 3mm pearl, a 15º seed bead, three 11º seed beads, and a 15º four times, leaving a 12" tail. Sew through the first pearl, 15º and three 11ºs **(fig. 1)**.

3. Arrange your triangle beads in a row so that they are all pointing up with their holes in a row at the bottom. Check to make sure all the holes are clear. If you are making multiple links, arrange enough triangles to do several, if not all, of your links.

4. Pick up a triangle, an 11º, and a triangle. Make sure you are going through two holes that are side-by-side in two triangles that are next to each other **(fig. 2)**.

fig. 1

fig. 2

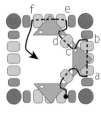

fig. 3

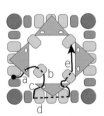

fig. 4

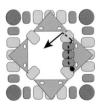

fig. 5

5. Sew through the next three 11ºs (**fig. 3, a–b**).

6. Sew through the free hole in the closest triangle **(c)**. Pick up an 11º and a triangle. Make sure all the triangles point the same way **(d)**. Sew through the next three 11ºs **(e–f)**. Repeat this step.

7. Sew through the free hole in the triangle you just picked up **(fig. 4, a)**. Pick up an 11º. Sew through the free hole in the remaining triangle **(b–c)**.

8. Sew through three 11ºs, a triangle, and an 11º **(d–e)**. *Pick up three 15ºs, and sew through the next 11º on the inside **(fig. 5)**. Repeat from the * three times. Sew through just the four sets of three 15ºs again to tighten them into a square.

9. Sew through an 11º, a triangle, a 15º, and two 11ºs **(fig. 6)**. (Stop here if you are making earrings or a bracelet. Continue to the next step to make a link.)

10. Pick up six 15ºs and an 11º, and sew through a soldered jump ring **(fig. 7, a–b)**. Sew back through the beads and continue through two 11ºs, a 15º, a pearl, a 15º, and two 11ºs **(c–d)**.

11. Pick up six 15ºs and an 11º, and sew through a soldered jump ring **(fig. 8, a–b)**. Sew back through the 11º and 15ºs. Continue through two 11ºs, a 15º, a pearl, a 15º, three 11ºs, a 15º, a pearl, a 15º, three 11ºs, a 15º, a pearl, a 15º, and two 11ºs **(c–d)**.

12. Pick up six 15ºs. Sew through an 11º and a soldered jump ring. Sew back through the 11º and the 15ºs you just picked up. Continue through two 11ºs, a 15º, a pearl, a 15º, and two 11ºs. Pick up six 15ºs. Sew through an 11º and a soldered jump ring. Sew back through the 11º and the 15ºs you just picked up. Secure both thread ends, and trim the excess thread.

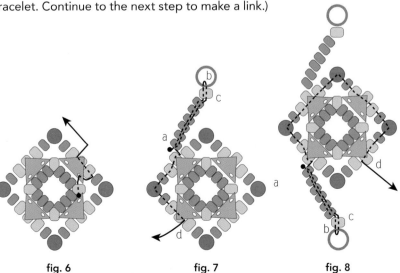

fig. 6   fig. 7

fig. 8

▲	Two-hole triangle
●	3mm crystal pearl
▢	11º seed bead
▬	15º seed bead

This graceful bezel can be made with either a 14mm crystal ring or a 14mm rivoli. From certain angles, the crystal gives the illusion of floating inside the setting—a rather magical touch.

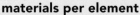

materials per element
- **14mm** crystal ring or rivoli
- **6** two-hole triangles
- **6** 3mm crystal pearls
- .5g **11º** seed beads
- .5g **15º** seed beads
- Size D nylon thread

tools
- Size 12 needles
- Silicon thread conditioner
- Thread snips

1. Stretch and condition approximately 5' thread, and thread a needle. Pick up a stop bead and slide it 14" from the end of the thread. Pick up two 11º seed beads and three 15º seed beads six times, and sew back through the first two 11ºs to form a ring **(fig. 1)**.

2. Arrange the triangle beads in a row with their holes in a row. If your triangles have a right side, place them right-side down. Always pick them up in the same way, either moving right to left or left to right. Pick up a triangle and two 11ºs, and sew through the free hole in the triangle. Sew through two 11ºs, three 15ºs, and two 11ºs **(fig. 2)**. The triangle will end up sandwiched between two pairs of 11ºs. Repeat five times, sewing on a total of six triangles. Continue through a triangle and two 11ºs. Set the needle aside.

3. Remove the stop bead and thread a needle on the tail. Sew through the center ring of 11ºs and 15ºs a few more times to tighten and strengthen it. Secure the thread with a couple of slip knots, and trim the excess thread.

4. With the original needle, pick up a 15º, an 11º, a pearl, an 11º, and a 15º. Sew through the two 11ºs on the outside of the next triangle **(fig. 3)**. Repeat five times. Continue through a 15º, an 11º, and a pearl.

5. Pick up three 15ºs, an 11º, a 15º, and an 11º. Skip the end 11º, and sew back through a 15º and an 11º **(fig. 4, a–b)**. Pick up three 15ºs and sew through the next pearl **(c–d)**. Repeat this step five times. Continue through three 15ºs, an 11º, a 15º and an 11º **(e–f)**.

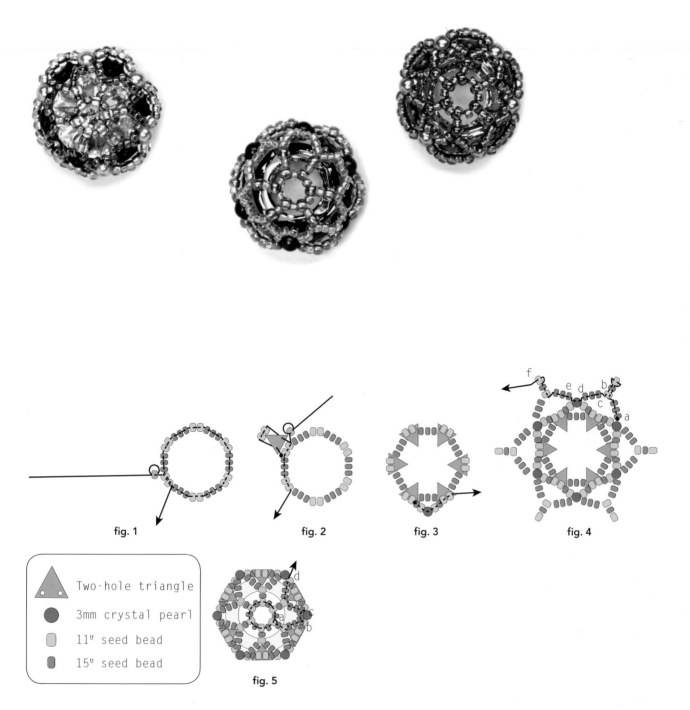

fig. 1

fig. 2

fig. 3

fig. 4

Two-hole triangle

3mm crystal pearl

11º seed bead

15º seed bead

fig. 5

6. Hold the crystal face up while you pick up a 15º and sew through the next 11º. Repeat five times **(fig. 5)**. Sew through the 11ºs and 15ºs a few more times to tighten the tension and make sure that this little ring will hold its shape. End by exiting an 11º. Continue through a 15º, an 11º, and three 15ºs **(a–b)**.

7. Pick up two 15ºs. Sew through three 15ºs so that the two 15ºs sit on top of a pearl. Skip an 11º, and sew through three 15ºs **(c–d)**. Repeat this step five times.

8. If you are going to be stringing the lattice, sew the thread in, securing it with a couple of slip knots. Trim the excess thread. Avoid the pairs of 11ºs on the outside of the triangles—you will be stringing through these. Otherwise, remove the needle and bundle your thread (Basics).

Adorn that inner child as she so richly deserves! The O-bead embellishments on the gently tilting triangles add visual interest and the fact the pinwheels are double-faced means that they look great from every angle.

materials per element
- **12** two-hole triangles
- **12** 3mm crystal pearls
- **24** O-beads
- **.5g** 11º seed beads
- **.75g** 15º seed beads
- **2** 4mm soldered jump rings
- Size D nylon thread

tools
- Size 12 needles
- Silicon thread conditioner
- Thread snips

If you can't find O-beads, substitute 3mm or 4mm heishi spacer beads.

1. Stretch and condition 4' thread, and thread a needle. String on a stop bead and slide it 14" from the end of the thread. Pick up 24 11º seed beads, and sew back through the first two to form a ring **(fig. 1)**. Arrange six triangles point up and face down. Arrange 12 O-beads face down.

2. Pick up a triangle from the right-hand hole, an O-bead, and an 11º **(fig. 2, a–b)**. Sew back through the O-bead and the triangle. Continue through the next two 11ºs **(c–d)**. Sew through the free hole in the triangle. Pick up an O-bead and an 11º **(fig. 3, a–b)**. Sew back through the O-bead and the triangle. Continue through the next two 11ºs **(c–d)**. Repeat this step five times. Continue through a triangle, an O-bead, and an 11º.

3. Pick up a pearl. Sew through the next 11º covering the same hole in the next triangle. Push the free 11ºs to the outside. Repeat five times. Continue through a pearl and an 11º **(fig. 4)**.

4. Pick up four 15º seed beads. Sew through the next 11º (use the same 11ºs as in step 3) **(fig. 5)**. Repeat this step five times. Sew through all the 15ºs and 11ºs to tighten your tension. End in an 11º. Sew through an O-bead, a triangle and two 11ºs under the triangle **(fig. 6)**.

5. Arrange six triangles point-down and face-down. Arrange 12 O-beads so they are face down. Repeat steps 2–4. Make sure you place these six triangles so that their points fall between the points of

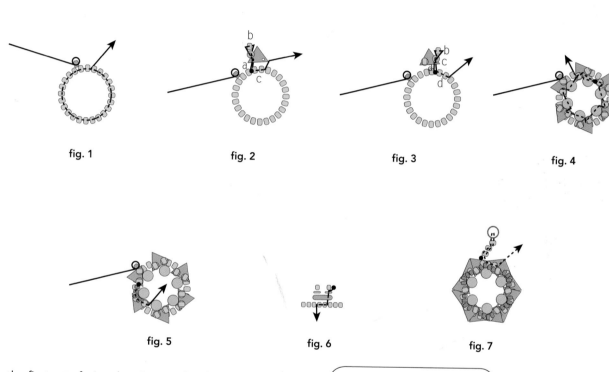

fig. 1   fig. 2   fig. 3   fig. 4

fig. 5   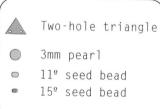 fig. 6   fig. 7

the first set of triangles. Secure the thread in the center pearls, 11ºs and 15ºs. Trim the excess thread.

▲	Two-hole triangle
●	3mm pearl
▢	11º seed bead
▬	15º seed bead

6. Remove the stop bead and thread a needle on the tail. Pick up three 11ºs, and sew through a soldered jump ring and back through the three 11ºs. Continue through two 11ºs in the center ring of seed beads **(fig. 7)**. Pick up two 11ºs. Sew through an 11º and the jump ring. Sew back through three 11ºs. Sew through the five 11ºs and two 11ºs from the original ring to strengthen the connection and tighten the tension. Sew through the center ring of 11ºs until you pass through the two 11ºs that are directly opposite the ones with the jump ring connection. Repeat if you need or want a second jump ring connection. Secure the thread in the center ring of 11ºs. Trim the excess thread.

you like the idea of including a hug and a kiss in
e making for someone important to you. It's a
y of putting your thoughts and feelings into a gift.

materials per element
- **4** brick beads
- **2** two-hole lentils
- **2** 3mm crystal pearls
- .25g 11º seed beads
- .25g 15º seed beads
- **2** 4mm soldered jump rings (optional)
- Size D nylon thread

tools
- Size 12 needles
- Silicon thread conditioner
- Thread snips

1. Stretch and condition approximately 3' thread, and thread on a size 12 needle.

2. Pick up a brick and an 11º four times. Sew back through the first brick so that the beads form a ring. Leave a 12" tail **(fig. 1)**.

3. Pick up an 11º and sew through a brick, an 11º, and a brick **(a–b)**. Pick up another 11º and sew through a brick and an 11º **(c)**.

4. Pick up three 15ºs, and sew through the free hole in the brick **(fig. 2, a)**. Pick up three 15ºs, and sew through either 11º **(b)**. Pick up three 15ºs, and sew through the

free hole in the brick **(c)**. Pick up three 15ºs, and sew through an 11º **(d)**. Repeat this step once. Set aside the needle and thread you have been working with. Thread a size 12 needle onto the tail.

5. Sew through an 11º, a brick, and an 11º without 15ºs. Pick up three 15ºs, and sew through a brick, three 15ºs, an 11º, three 15ºs, and a brick **(fig. 3, a–b)**. Pick up three 15ºs, and sew through the 11º with no 15ºs **(c–d)**. Pick up three 15ºs, and sew through a brick, three 15ºs, an 11º, three 15ºs, and a brick **(fig. 4, a–b)**. Pick up three 15ºs, and sew through the 11º with only one set of 15ºs **(c–d)**.

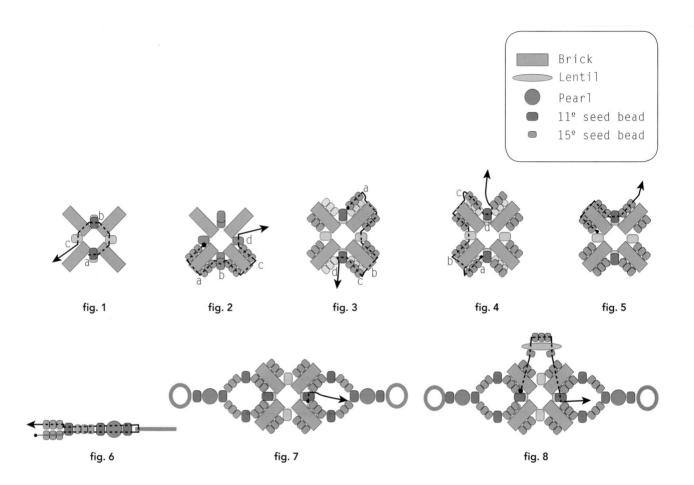

Brick
Lentil
Pearl
11º seed bead
15º seed bead

fig. 1

fig. 2

fig. 3

fig. 4

fig. 5

fig. 6

fig. 7

fig. 8

6. Switch back to the original needle and thread. Sew through three 15ºs, a brick, three 15ºs, an 11º, and three 15ºs (**fig. 5**).

7. Pick up an 11º, three 15ºs, an 11º, a pearl, and an 11º, and sew through a soldered jump ring. Sew back through the beads you picked up. After the 11º, continue through the three 15ºs that are not already connected to the beads you picked up (**fig. 6**). Continue through an 11º and three 15ºs. Pick up an 11º and three 15ºs, and sew through an 11º, a pearl, an 11º and the jump ring. Sew back through the 11º, the pearl, the 11º, and the beads you picked up. After the 11º, continue through the three 15ºs that are not attached to the jump ring linkage.

8. Weave to the other side of the link and out through a doubled set of three 15ºs as shown previously in fig. 5.

9. Repeat step 7. Continue through an 11º (**fig. 7**).

10. Pick up a 15º, a lentil, and three 15ºs. Sew through the free hole in the lentil. Pick up a 15º. Sew through the 11º directly across from the one where you started this step (**fig. 8**). Sew through the beads two more times to tighten the tension.

11. Sew through the link so that you bring your needle out through one of the doubled 11ºs on the other side of the link. Repeat step 10 to place a second lentil bridge on the link.

12. The beadwork is very tight, so weave your threads in as best you can, hiding any slip knots in the bricks.

Wake up and see the style when you put some coffee beans in your design. This is a very versatile element for jewelry: You can weave this link together to make straps, use it as a link between other elements, make a pair of earrings, or even use it as a charm. Its classic lines make the Coffee Bean Link an asset in many styles.

materials per element
- **8** two-hole lentils
- **4** berry beads
- **.25g** 11º seed beads
- **.25g** 15º seed beads
- Size D nylon thread

tools
- Size 12 needles
- Silicon thread conditioner
- Thread snips

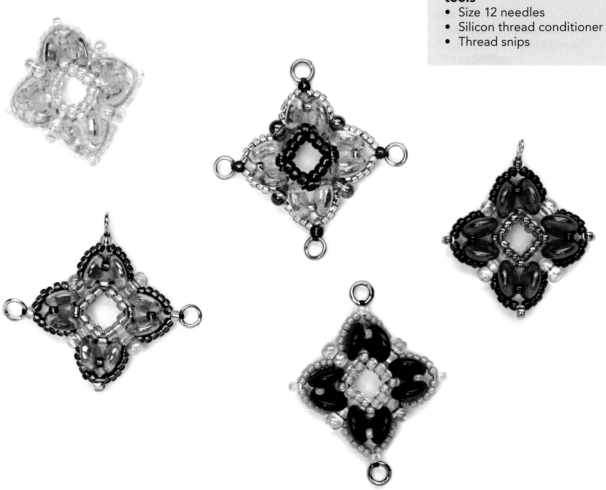

1. Stretch and condition 3' thread. Thread a needle on one end. Pick up 16 11º seed beads. Sew back through the first four 11ºs to form a ring **(fig. 1)**.

2. Pick up a lentil and three 15º seed beads, and sew through the free hole in the lentil **(fig. 2, a–b)**. Pick up a 15º, a lentil, and three 15ºs, and sew through the free hole in the lentil **(c–d)**. Continue through five 11ºs, so the first one is sandwiched between the lentils **(e)**. Repeat this step three times, and continue through a lentil and three 15ºs **(fig. 3)**. (If you prefer, you can use an 11º in place of the 15º between the lentils.)

3. Set aside your needle, and thread a needle on the tail. Sew through the twelve 11ºs in the center ring. Skip the 11ºs sandwiched between lentils. Secure your thread with a few slip knots. Trim the excess tail thread.

4. At this point, you need to know how you will be using the link. For every jump ring you need, refer to A. If you do not need a jump ring, refer to B.
A. With the original needle, pick up three 15ºs and an 11º, and sew through a jump ring and back through the 11º **(fig. 4, a–b)**. Pick up three 15ºs and sew through three 15ºs **(c–d)**. Pick up a berry bead and sew through three 15ºs **(e–f)**.

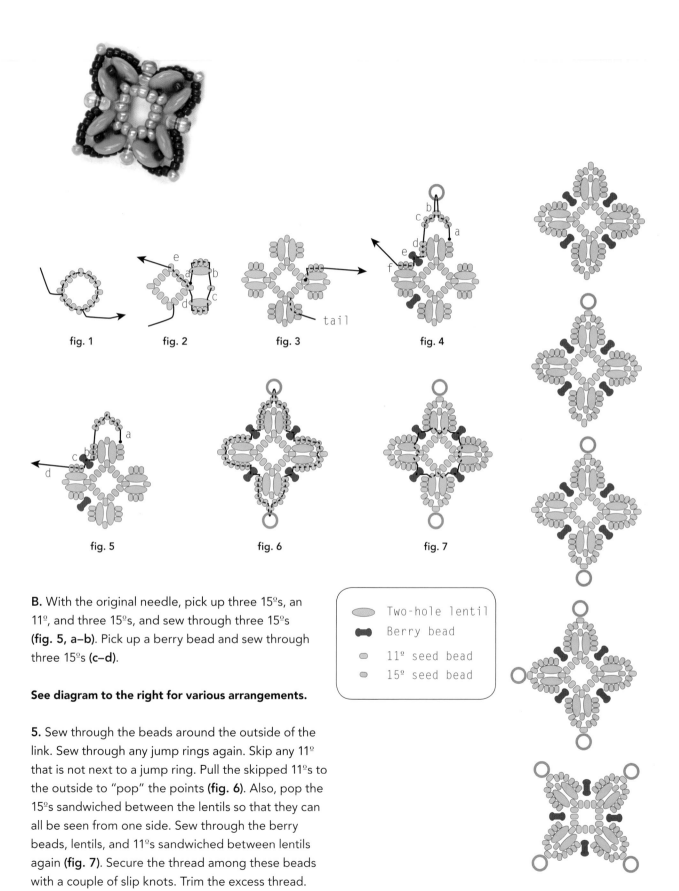

fig. 1

fig. 2

fig. 3

tail

fig. 4

fig. 5

fig. 6

fig. 7

B. With the original needle, pick up three 15⁰s, an 11⁰, and three 15⁰s, and sew through three 15⁰s **(fig. 5, a–b)**. Pick up a berry bead and sew through three 15⁰s **(c–d)**.

See diagram to the right for various arrangements.

5. Sew through the beads around the outside of the link. Sew through any jump rings again. Skip any 11⁰ that is not next to a jump ring. Pull the skipped 11⁰s to the outside to "pop" the points **(fig. 6)**. Also, pop the 15⁰s sandwiched between the lentils so that they can all be seen from one side. Sew through the berry beads, lentils, and 11⁰s sandwiched between lentils again **(fig. 7)**. Secure the thread among these beads with a couple of slip knots. Trim the excess thread.

Two-hole lentil
Berry bead
11⁰ seed bead
15⁰ seed bead

DIAGRAM

Made with a cross-weaving technique, this whimsical link looks a lot like a fancy tied bow. Think about including one (or more) when you make a gift, because nothing dresses up a present like a gorgeous bow!

materials per element
- **3** two-hole daggers
- **2** petal beads
- **3** two-hole lentils
- .25g 11º seed beads
- .75g 15º seed beads
- **1** or **2** 4mm soldered jump rings
- Size D nylon thread

tools
- Size 12 needles
- Silicon thread conditioner
- Thread snips

	Two-hole dagger
	Petal bead
	Two-hole lentil
	11º seed bead
	15º seed bead

Most of the time, two size 12 needles can pass through 11º beads and daggers simultaneously. This is a real advantage with crossweave techniques.

1. Stretch and condition 4' of thread, and center the thread on a soldered jump ring with a lark's head knot (Basics). Thread a needle on each end. Sew through an 11º seed bead with both needles heading in the same direction **(fig. 1, a)**. Pick up four 15ºs, and repeat with the second needle **(b)**. Sew through the longer hole in a dagger, with both needles heading in opposite directions **(c)**. Reinforce the thread paths by sewing back through everything again. End with the needles in the positions shown in **fig. 1, point c**.

2. On one needle, pick up three 15ºs **(fig. 2, a)**, and sew through the narrow hole in the dagger **(b)**. Repeat with the second needle **(c–d)**. Reinforce the thread paths made in this step. When done, both needles must be exiting the dagger's top hole, heading in opposite directions **(b, d)**.

3. On one needle, pick up a 15º, a dagger (through the long hole), and three 15ºs, and sew through the free hole in the dagger **(fig. 3, a–b)**. Repeat with the second needle **(c–d)**. Sew through a 15º, an 11º, and a 15º with both needles heading in opposite directions **(c)**. Reinforce the thread path. End with each needle exiting the small hole in a dagger, next to a 15º **(fig. 4)**.

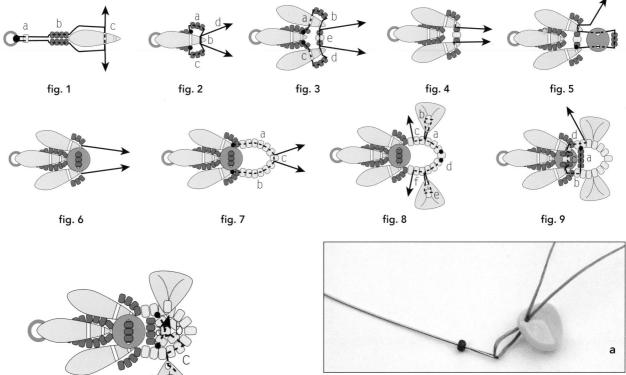

fig. 1   fig. 2   fig. 3   fig. 4   fig. 5

fig. 6   fig. 7   fig. 8   fig. 9

fig. 10

4. Pick up on one needle a lentil and three 15⁰s. Sew through the free hole in the lentil and the small hole in a dagger so that the lentil sits on top of a 15⁰, an 11⁰, and a 15⁰ **(fig. 5)**. With the second needle, sew through a lentil, three 15⁰s, the second hole in the lentil and the small hole in a dagger. You should have a needle and thread on the outside of each dagger **(fig. 6)**.

5. On one needle, pick up a 15⁰ and six 11⁰s **(fig. 7, a)**. Repeat with the other needle **(b)**. Sew through an 11⁰ with both needles heading in opposite directions **(c)**.

6. Sew one needle through three 11⁰s. Pick up a petal from the back and an 11⁰ **(photo a and fig. 8, a)**. Sew through the petal **(b)**. Continue through two 11⁰s, heading toward the daggers **(c)**. Repeat with the second needle **(d–f)**.

7. It is easier to do this step and part of the next one from the back. Pick up on one needle four 15⁰s **(fig. 9, a)**. Sew through an 11⁰, a 15⁰, and a dagger **(b)**. Pick up a 15⁰ and sew through an 11⁰. Pick up a 15⁰ and sew through a dagger, a 15⁰, and two 11⁰s **(c–d)**. With

the second needle, sew through four 15⁰s, an 11⁰, a 15⁰, a dagger, a 15⁰, an 11⁰, a 15⁰, a dagger, a 15⁰, and two 11⁰s. (This is the same thread path as shown in **fig. 9**).

8. Pick up an 11⁰. Pick up an 11⁰ with the second needle. Sew both needles through an 11⁰, going in opposite directions **(fig. 10, a)**. With one needle, pick up an 11⁰ **(b)**, and sew through two 11⁰s **(photo b)**. Continue through a petal and the 11⁰ in front of the petal **(c–d)**. With the second needle, pick up an 11⁰, and sew through two 11⁰s **(photo c)**. Continue through a petal and the 11⁰ in front of the petal—this is a mirror image of the thread path shown in **fig. 10**.

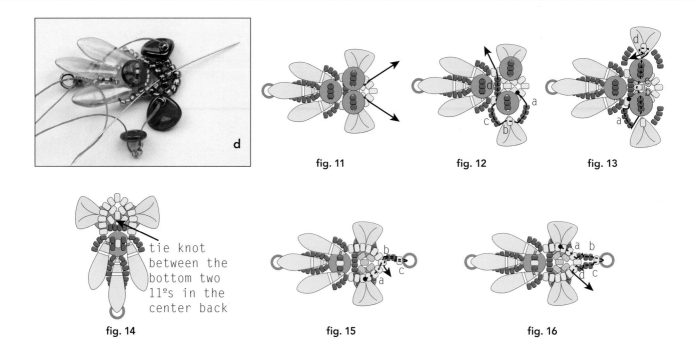

d

fig. 11   fig. 12   fig. 13

tie knot
between the
bottom two
11ºs in the
center back

fig. 14   fig. 15   fig. 16

9. With one needle, pick up a lentil and three 15ºs, and sew through the free hole in the lentil. Pick up a 15º and sew through two 11ºs **(photo d)**. Repeat with the second needle **(fig. 11)**.

10. With one needle, pick up four 15ºs. Sew through the 11º on top of a petal **(fig. 12, a–b)**. Pick up another four 15ºs and sew through the four 15ºs at the fairy's waist **(c–d)**. Repeat with the second needle.

11. With one needle, sew through four 15ºs, a lentil, and three 15ºs **(fig. 13, a–b)**. Pick up an 11º and sew through three 15ºs, a lentil, an 11º, and a petal **(c–d)**. With the second needle, sew through four 15ºs, a lentil, three 15ºs, and SKIP the 11º. Sew through three 15ºs, a lentil, an 11º, and a petal. Pull on both threads and squeeze the lentils together in the middle to help define the Flower Fairy's bosom.

12A. If you do not yet know how the Flower Fairy attaches, bundle the threads (Basics).

12B. If your Flower Fairy will be stitched to another element, weave both threads in, securing them with a couple of slip knots. Avoid the 11º at the center top. I know this is considered very bad form, but I found it handy to weave the threads to meet as shown in **fig. 14**, tie them together, and weave into the skirt before trimming the excess.

12C. If you are attaching another jump ring or sewing the element onto a jump ring: Sew through four 11ºs **(fig. 15, a)**, pick up two 15ºs and an 11º, and sew through a soldered jump ring and back through the 11º and two 15ºs. Continue through the center top 11º **(b–c)**, pick up two 15ºs, and sew through the 11º and the jump ring. Sew back through the 11º, the 15ºs you just picked up, and the center 11º. With the second needle, sew through three 15ºs **(fig. 16, a)**, pick up a 15º, and sew through two 15ºs, an 11º, a jump ring, an 11º, and the other two 15ºs **(b–c)**. Pick up a 15º and sew through an 11º next to the center top 11º **(d)**. Weave both threads in, securing them with a couple of slip knots. Trim the excess thread.

This link is useful for connecting two large or stiff elements and adding some flexibility to the joint. This is often the last element you will make for a project.

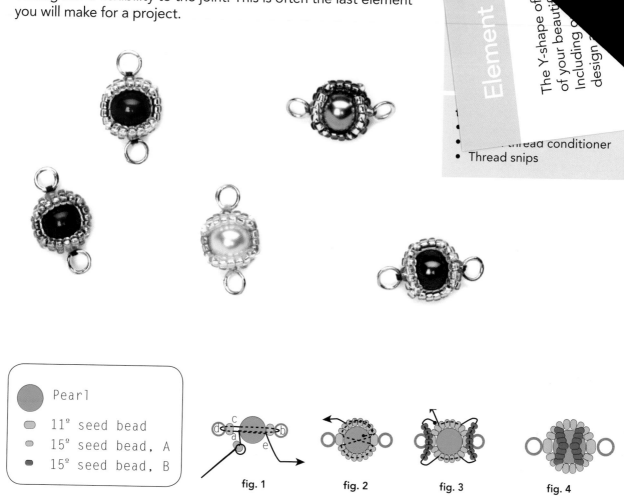

Pearl

○ 11º seed bead

○ 15º seed bead, A

● 15º seed bead, B

fig. 1

fig. 2

fig. 3

fig. 4

1. Stretch and condition approximately 3' of thread, and thread a size 12 needle on one end. String on a stop bead and slide it 8" from the tail. Pick up a 6mm pearl and an 11º seed bead, and sew through a soldered jump ring and back through the beads **(fig. 1, a–c)**. Pick up an 11º, sew through another soldered jump ring, and sew back through the 11º and the pearl **(d–e)**.

2. Pick up eight color A 15º seed beads, and sew through the pearl so that the beads stretch from hole to hole. Repeat. Sew through six As **(fig. 2)**.

3. Pick up seven color B 15º seed beads, and sew through the center four As in the other line of As **(photo)**. Repeat so you have two color B stripes lying across the pearl **(fig. 3)**. Repeat two more times to make two stripes of B beads on each side of the pearl **(fig. 4)**.

4. Sew through two As, a pearl, and an 11º. Sew through the jump ring and weave through to the other end of the link. Reinforce the thread around the jump ring at this end. Weave the needle to meet the tail and tie the two ends together. Pull the ends through the 11ºs and the pearl. Trim the excess thread.

This component allows it to heighten the effect
...ul pendant in either a strung or beadwoven design.
...ne of these unusual shapes as an element in your
...adds a touch of sophistication.

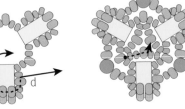

materials per element
- **3** brick beads
- **3** 3mm crystal pearls, color P
- **3** 3mm crystal pearls, color C
- **.5g** 11º seed beads
- **.5g** 15º seed beads, color F
- **.25g** 15ºs, color G
- Size D nylon thread

tools
- Size 12 and 13 needles
- Silicon thread conditioner
- Thread snips

1. Stretch and condition 4' thread, and thread a size 12 needle on one end. Pick up a brick, two 15º seed beads, an 11º seed bead, and two 15ºs three times. Sew back through the first brick so that the beads form a ring. Leave a 12" tail **(fig. 1)**.

You will use color F 15ºs exclusively until the last step of the component. Color F 15ºs will be referred to as 15º in the instructions, without any other designation. Do not use the color G 15ºs until directed to do so.

2. Pick up a 15º, an 11º, and a 15º. Sew through the free hole in the brick **(fig. 2, a)**. Pick up a 15º, an 11º, and a 15º, and sew through a brick, two 15ºs, an 11º, two 15ºs, and a brick **(b–c)**. Repeat this step two times. Continue through two 15ºs, an 11º, three 15ºs, an 11º, and a 15º **(d–e)**.

3. Pick up a 15º, two 11ºs and a 15º, and sew through the 15º, 11º, and 15º on the other side of the brick **(fig. 3, a–b)**. Continue sewing through two 15ºs, an 11º, three 15ºs, an 11º, and a 15º **(c–d)**. Repeat this step

fig. 1

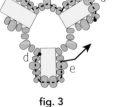

fig. 2

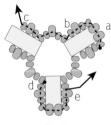

fig. 3

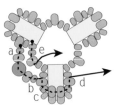

fig. 4

fig. 5

twice, keeping the seed bead loops on the same side of the beadwork. Continue through a 15º, two 11ºs, two 15ºs, and an 11º **(e)**. Your needle must be heading into the center as you exit the last 11º.

4. Pick up a 15º, an 11º, a color C pearl, an 11º, and a 15º. Sew through the 11º along the side of the next brick heading out from the center **(fig. 4, a–b)**. Pick up a 15º, two 11ºs, and a 15º. Sew through the 11º on the other side of this same brick heading into the center **(c–d)**. Repeat this step twice, and continue through a 15º, an 11º, and a pearl. Set this needle and thread aside. Thread a needle onto the tail, and sew through two 15ºs and an 11º **(e)**.

5. Still working with the tail thread, pick up two 15ºs, an 11º, and two 15ºs, and sew through the next 11º between bricks **(photo a)**. Repeat twice, and continue through two 15ºs and an 11º **(fig. 5)**. Sew through only the three 11ºs, pulling them into the center. Secure the tail thread in the original ring of beads. Don't place any knots in the center three 11ºs. Trim the excess thread.

6. Using the original needle and thread, pick up two 15ºs, and sew through the nearest center 11º **(photo b)**. Pick up two 15ºs and sew through the next pearl. Repeat this step twice, pinching in the pearls as you go to draw them into the center. Continue through two 15ºs, skip an 11º, and continue through two more 15ºs **(fig. 6)**.

7. Pick up three 15ºs, sew through two 15ºs, skip an 11º, and sew through two 15ºs. Repeat twice, and continue through three 15ºs **(photo c)**. Pick up a color P pearl, and sew through three 15ºs **(fig. 7, a–b)**. Sew in two more Ps, and continue through a pearl **(c)**. Sew through just the pearls to draw them together. Sew 15ºs of either color between the pearls—just use the same color all the time **(fig. 8)**. After sewing through the last pearl, continue through three 15ºs **(fig. 8, a–b)**.

8. Pick up four color G 15ºs and sew through three Fs **(fig. 9, a–b)**. Repeat twice. Weave the thread in—you probably will have to hide your slip knots in the pearls or inside the groups of four Gs. Trim the excess thread.

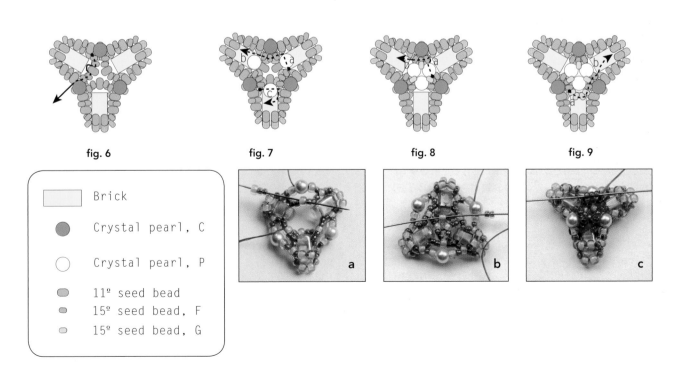

fig. 6   fig. 7   fig. 8   fig. 9

▭	Brick
●	Crystal pearl, C
○	Crystal pearl, P
◓	11º seed bead
●	15º seed bead, F
⬭	15º seed bead, G

a   b   c

You will love the way the crystal drop winks at you as the Crown Jewel twists in your design. As an earring, it's elegant; when added as embellishment, it's opulent.

materials per element
- 12x8 crystal drop
- **6** SuperDuos, color A
- **3** SuperDuos, color B
- 6mm crystal pearl or bicone
- 4mm crystal pearl or bicone
- **2** 3mm fancy spacers
- 2.5mm round metal bead
- **9** 11º seed beads
- .25g 15º seed beads, color E
- .5g 15ºs, color F
- 5mm bead cap
- 3" 22-gauge headpin
- Size D nylon thread

tools
- Size 12 and 13 needles
- Silicon thread conditioner
- Thread snips
- Chainnose pliers
- Roundnose pliers
- Flush cutters
- Cheater tool/1mm tapered nose pliers

1. Stretch and condition 4' thread, and thread a size 12 needle onto one end. Pick up a color B SuperDuo, an 11º seed bead, a color A SuperDuo, and an 11º three times. Sew through the first B so the beads form a circle. Center the beads on the thread, ignoring the position of the needle **(fig. 1)**.

You are more likely to use Chinese crystal drops than any other kind—they are easy to find in this size. However, they are not always consistent in size. Be careful to pick two that are the same length and have tips shaped the same.

2. Pick up two color E 15º seed beads. Sew through the free hole in the B **(fig. 2, a–b)**. Pick up two Es. Sew through a B, an 11º, an A, an 11º, and a B **(c–d)**. Repeat step 2 twice. Sew through two more Es and a B **(fig. 3)**.

3. Begin pulling the Bs together: Pick up two Es, and sew through the next B **(fig. 4, a–b)**. Repeat twice. Sew through the first two 15ºs between Bs. *Pick up three color F 15º seed beads. Sew through the next two Es connecting the B **(c–d)**.* Repeat the section between the * two more times, and then continue through an F.

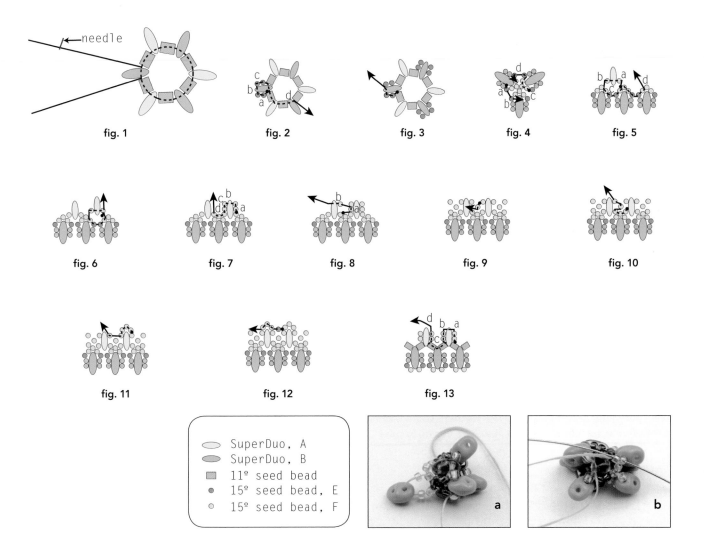

fig. 1

fig. 2

fig. 3

fig. 4

fig. 5

fig. 6

fig. 7

fig. 8

fig. 9

fig. 10

fig. 11

fig. 12

fig. 13

needle

◯ SuperDuo, A
◖ SuperDuo, B
▢ 11º seed bead
● 15º seed bead, E
○ 15º seed bead, F

a

b

4. Pick up an F, an A, and an F **(fig. 5, a–b)**. Sew through an F, two Es, three Fs, two Es, and an F. The Fs and A sit above color Es **(c–d, photo a)**. Repeat this step once.

5. Pick up an F, an A, and an F. Sew through an F, two Es, and two Fs **(fig. 6)**. Note that the last F you sew through is the one you just picked up **(photo b)**.

6. Pick up two Fs, and sew through the free hole in the A **(fig. 7, a–b)**.

7. Pick up two Fs, and sew through three Fs **(c–d)**. Sew through the second F from the top of the A **(fig. 8, a)**. Pick up an F, and sew through the free hole in the A **(b)**. Repeat this step once.

8. Pick up an F, and sew through the second F from the top, heading towards the Bs **(fig. 9, photo c)**. Sew through five F **(fig. 10)**.

9. Pick up three Fs, and sew through two Fs **(fig. 11)**. Repeat twice. Sew through the first three Fs you picked up in this step.

10. Pick up an E, and sew through three Fs **(fig. 12)**. Repeat twice. Pass through just the Fs again. Make sure the thread goes behind the Es so they get pushed forward. Weave in the working thread a short distance and secure it with a slip knot or two. Trim the excess thread. Switch your needle to the remaining tail. Make sure the thread is exiting an 11º bead, heading toward an A.

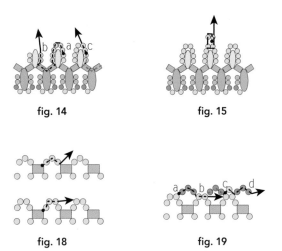

fig. 14   fig. 15

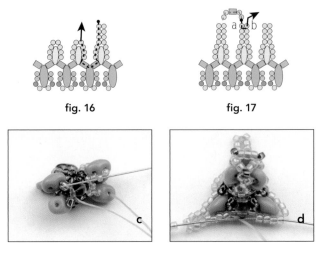

fig. 16   fig. 17

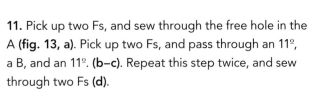

fig. 18   fig. 19

11. Pick up two Fs, and sew through the free hole in the A (**fig. 13, a**). Pick up two Fs, and pass through an 11º, a B, and an 11º. (**b–c**). Repeat this step twice, and sew through two Fs (**d**).

Thread tends to show a lot with the stitch used at step 12 (herringbone), so it is a good idea to work this stitch from the back. Also, don't pull the thread tightly. You will sew round and round, and sew through some beads a lot. If your tension is relaxed, it will be easier to pass through the beads multiple times.

12. Pick up four Fs, and sew through two Fs, an 11º, a B, an 11º, and two Fs (**fig. 14, a–b**). Repeat twice, and sew through two more Fs (**c**).

13. Pick up two Fs. *Sew down through one F and up through two Fs (**fig. 15**).* Repeat the section between * twice. Sew through seven Fs, an 11º, a B, an 11º, and four Fs (**fig. 16**). Repeat the entire step twice. Continue through four Fs and exit an end bead in one of the bars.

You may find it too difficult to go through the 11º–SuperDuo–11º section when you finish one bar and move to do the next. If you do, try this alternative: sew through the Fs at the end as directed, ending with the two along the side of the SuperDuo. Pick up four Fs. Sew through four Fs (photo d). After you complete the third bar, you will pick up four Fs and sew through seven Fs.

14. Pick up three Fs, an 11º, and three Fs. Sew down through one F in the next herringbone column (**fig. 17, a**). Sew up through the 15º next to the one you sewed down through (**b**). Repeat from the beginning of this step once. Pop in a crystal drop, with the wide end next to the SuperDuos. Then repeat from the beginning again. Sew through three Fs and an 11º.

15. Pick up three Fs (four if you are using a Chinese crystal drop), and sew through an 11º. Repeat twice. Sew through three Fs no matter what kind of drop you have (**fig. 18**). Skip to step 17 if you have a Chinese drop.

16. Pick up an E and sew through three Fs. Repeat twice. Weave in tail enough to secure it. Trim the excess thread. Skip to step 18.

17. Pick up three Es. Sew through the center two Fs of the next group of four Fs (**fig. 19, a–b**). Repeat twice. Sew through three Es, pick up an F, and sew through three Es (**c–d**). Repeat twice. Weave once more just through the Es. Make sure the thread goes behind the Fs so that they are pushed to the outside. Weave in the tail to secure it and trim the excess thread.

18. Stack on a headpin: a 4mm crystal pearl, a 3mm spacer, a beaded jewel (point down), a 3mm spacer, a 6mm crystal pearl, a bead cap, and a 2.5mm metal bead. Make a wrapped loop to connect the Crown Jewel Drop to a project (Basics).

Include a swag if you want an extra-dramatic pendant with your Sunburst (p. 8). A Sunburst Swag has a more organic feel to it, but that doesn't lessen the impact at all.

materials per element
- Sunburst, 9-point
- **6** or **7** two-hole daggers
- **4** 4mm bicones
- **4** 3mm crystal pearls
- **10** 11º seed beads*
- **8** 15º seed beads, color F
- .25g 15ºs, color G
- Size D nylon thread

tools
- Size 12 and 13 needles
- Thread snips

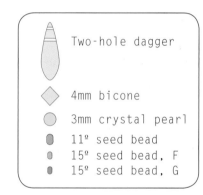

Two-hole dagger

4mm bicone

3mm crystal pearl

11º seed bead

15º seed bead, F

15º seed bead, G

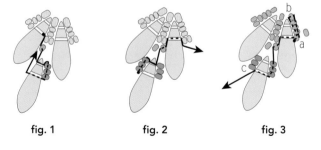

fig. 1   fig. 2   fig. 3

1. Unbundle your thread and straighten it, if necessary. Condition the thread and thread a needle onto the thread. *Pick up a color F 15º seed bead and a dagger, sewing through the hole closest to the tip. Pick up three color G 15ºs. Sew through the free hole in the dagger **(fig. 1)**. Pick up three Gs, and sew through the tip hole of the dagger. Pick up an F, and sew through the next dagger **(fig. 2)**.* Repeat the section between the * twice.

2. Sew through five Fs (you will be exiting a point) **(fig. 3, a–b)**. Sew back through four 15ºs, the dagger, an F, three Gs, and a dagger **(b–c)**. Note that the F you sew through after the dagger is one from step 1, not in the original Sunburst.

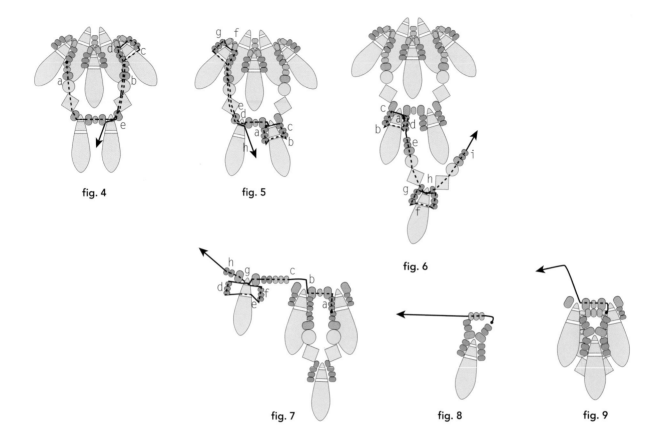

fig. 4

fig. 5

fig. 6

fig. 7

fig. 8

fig. 9

3. Pick up two Fs, an 11º, a pearl, a bicone, an 11º, a dagger tip, an 11º, an F, an 11º, a dagger tip, an 11º, a bicone, a pearl, an 11º, and two Fs **(fig. 4, a–b)**. Skip over the middle dagger in the swag, and sew through the long hole of the third dagger in the swag, three Gs, the tip hole, three Gs, two Fs, a pearl, a bicone, an 11º, and a dagger **(c–e)**.

4. Pick up three Gs, and sew through the free hole in the dagger **(fig. 5, a–b)**. Pick up three Gs, and sew through the tip hole, an 11º, a 15º, an 11º, and a dagger **(c–d)**. Continue sewing through an 11º, a bicone, a pearl, an 11º, two Fs, three Gs, and a dagger **(e–f)**. Continue through three Gs, a dagger, two Fs, an 11º, a pearl, a bicone, an 11º, and a dagger **(g–h)**.

5. Pick up three Gs, and sew through the free hole in the dagger **(fig. 6, a–b)**. Pick up three Gs, and sew through the dagger tip and three Gs **(c–d)**. Pick up two Gs, an 11º, a pearl, a bicone, a G, a dagger tip, and three Gs, and sew through the free hole in the dagger **(e–f)**. Pick up three Gs, and sew through the tip hole **(g–h)**. Pick up a G, a bicone, a pearl, an 11º, and two Gs **(i)**. If you do not wish to add the seventh dagger,

sew through the first three Gs, 11º, 15º, and 11º as shown in **fig. 7, a–b**. Secure your thread and trim the excess thread.

6. Sew through three Gs, an 11º, an F 15º, and an 11º **(fig. 7, a–b)**. Pick up three Fs, two Gs, an 11º, a dagger tip, and three Gs, and sew through the free hole in the dagger **(c–e)**. Pick up three Gs, and sew through the dagger tip **(f–g)**. Pick up an 11º and two Gs **(h)**.

7. Sew through three Fs so the beads form a loop **(fig. 8)**. Lay the three Fs on the beadwork so that they are parallel to the 11º, F, and 11º connecting two daggers **(fig. 9)**. Starting with the nearest 11º, sew through an 11º, F, and 11º. Weave the thread in a short distance, securing it with a couple of slip knots. Trim the excess thread.

Use one or two of these sturdy bars to include the Sunbursts (p. 8) in your designs. Simple but attractive, it doesn't detract from the beauty of the Sunburst.

materials per element
- Sunburst, 8- or 9-point
- 4mm bicone
- **2** 11º seed beads
- **16** 15º seed beads, color F
- **8** 15ºs, color G
- 4mm soldered jump ring
- Size D nylon thread

tools
- Size 12 and 13 needles
- Thread snips

◇ 4mm bicone

◦ 11º seed bead

◦ 15º seed bead, F

◦ 15º seed bead, G

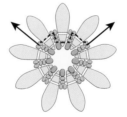

fig. 1

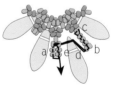

fig. 2

This is one of the few projects where I had to resort to a size 13 needle a couple of times. I didn't have to for every bar, but you may find yourself needing it.

1. Unbundle your thread and condition it. Thread on a size 12 needle and sew through a 15º seed bead.

If you have no thread because you have already used it to add a swag, then stretch and condition 1 yd. of thread. Thread a size 12 needle onto each end. Sew through the tip hole of a dagger. Center the thread.

Sew one needle through three color F 15ºs, a dagger, and an F. Repeat with the second needle. Set aside one needle until you are ready to complete the second bar (fig. 1).

2. Pick up four color F 15º seed beads, and sew through an F, a dagger, and an F (fig. 2, a–b). Sew through four Fs. You will be exiting a point (b–c). Sew back through four Fs, a dagger, and three Fs (c–e).

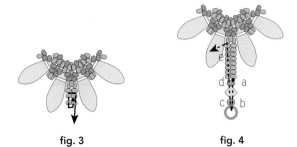

fig. 3

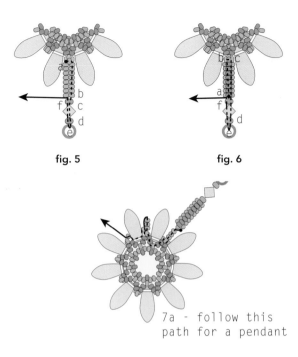

fig. 4

fig. 5

fig. 6

3. Pick up two Fs, and sew down through one F and up through another F **(fig. 3)**. Repeat five times. You will end up with two columns with eight beads in them; don't count the Fs that were part of the original Sunburst.

4. Pick up an 11º, a bicone, and an 11º **(fig. 4, a–b)**. Sew through a soldered jump ring and back through the 11º, bicone, and 11º **(c–d)** . Note which column your thread is coming out of—continue through all the 15ºs in the other column **(e)**.

5. Pick up an F, and sew up through all the beads in the column you did not come down **(fig. 5, a–b)**. Continue through the 11º, the bicone, and the second 11º **(c–d)**. Sew through the jump ring and back through the 11º, bicone, and 11º **(e–f)**.

6. Pick up eight color G 15º seed beads. Sew through the single F at the base of the columns **(fig. 6, a–b)**, and continue back through the Gs. Sew through an 11º, a bicone, and an 11º **(c–d)**, and sew through the jump ring and back through an 11º, bicone, and 11º **(e–f)**.

7. If this is your only bar, you can weave in the thread and trim the excess. You can hide it in the bar; believe me, that thread is not going anywhere. Also, weave in this thread if you started a double-ended thread in step 1. If you need a second bar, weave this thread into position using **figures 7a and 7b** as a guide. The easiest way to go across the Sunburst is to weave up through the 15ºs connecting the daggers to the top, then into the seed beads on top and through them to the appropriate place.

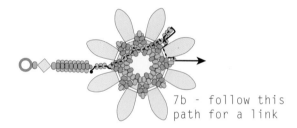

7a - follow this
path for a pendant

fig. 7a

7b - follow this
path for a link

fig. 7b

You can dress up any 24 or 25mm cabochon, donut, or bead with this bezel. The bead must be flat like a large coin or domed; spheres won't work. Pair the bezel with the Trefoil connector for a striking (and stringable) pendant, or include the optional bail to suspend the pendant from a simple cord necklace. You can even consider a micro-kumihimo or macramé cord for one of these pendants with a bail.

materials per element
- 24–25mm cabochon, donut, or bead
- **4** two-hole brick beads
- **12** berry beads
- **8** 3mm crystal pearls
- .75g 11º seed beads
- .75g 15º seed beads
- Size D nylon thread

tools
- Size 10 and 12 needles
- Silicon thread conditioner
- Thread snips

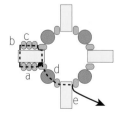

1. Stretch and condition 5' thread (6' to include the bail). Pick up a brick, an 11º seed bead, a pearl, and an 11º four times, and sew back through the first brick so that the beads form a ring. Leave a 15" tail **(fig. 1)**.

fig. 1

▭	Brick
●	3mm crystal pearl
▬	Berry bead
○	11º seed bead
●	15º seed bead

47

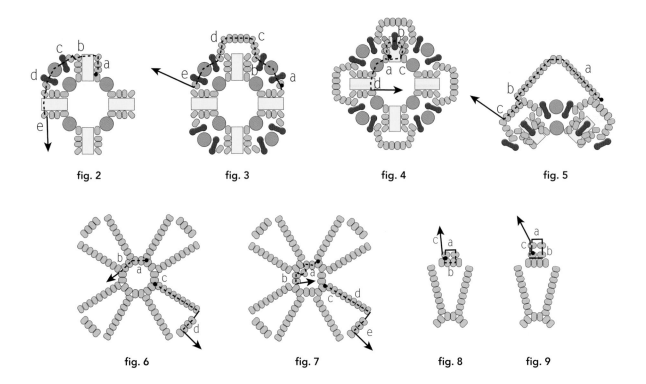

fig. 2   fig. 3   fig. 4   fig. 5

fig. 6   fig. 7   fig. 8   fig. 9

2. Pick up three 15ºs, and sew through the free hole in the brick **(a–b)**. Pick up three 15ºs, and sew through a brick, an 11º, a pearl, an 11º, and a brick **(c–e)**. Repeat this step three times **(fig. 2)**. Continue through three 15ºs, a brick, and a 15º **(a–b)**.

3. Pick up an 11º, a berry, a pearl, a berry, and an 11º. Sew through a 15º, a brick, and a 15º **(c–e)**. Repeat three times **(fig. 3)**. Continue through an 11º, a berry, a pearl, a berry, and an 11º **(a–b)**.

4. Pick up three 15ºs, four 11ºs, and three 15ºs, and sew through an 11º, a berry, a pearl, a berry, and an 11º **(c–e)**. Repeat three times, and continue through three 15ºs and four 11ºs. Set this needle aside. Thread a needle on the tail, pick up a 15º, an 11º, a berry, an 11º, and a 15º, and sew through a brick, an 11º, a pearl, an 11º, and a brick so that the berry sits on top of a brick **(fig. 4)**. Repeat this step three more times. Weave the tail in, securing it with a couple of slip knots. Trim the excess tail thread.

5. Resume weaving with the original needle to begin working on the back of the bezel. Pick up nine 15ºs, two 11ºs, and nine 15ºs, and sew through the next four 11ºs **(fig. 5)**. Repeat three times, and continue through nine 15ºs and two 11ºs.

Closing the back may take a little trial and error. I needed anywhere from one to four 11ºs for step 6, even when I used identical cabochons in different projects. Minor variations in the 15º production runs make important differences, as does the relative flatness of your bead or cabochon. Pick up the same number as you did the first time for every repetition. If you must pick up different numbers of beads in step 6, pick up the same number for sides opposite each other, such as 3–2–3–2.

6. Pick up two 11ºs, and sew through two 11ºs **(fig. 6)**. Repeat three times, wrapping the long loops to the back as you go. If the fit is too tight or too loose, undo the stitching and try again with a different count.

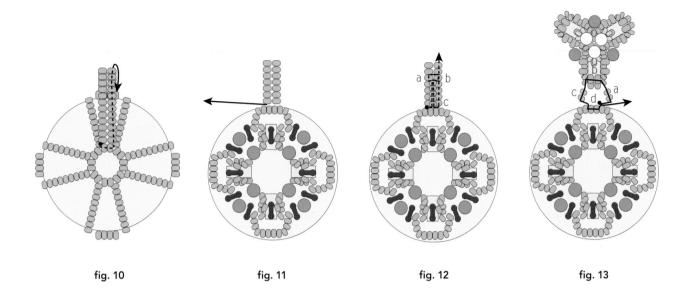

fig. 10   fig. 11   fig. 12   fig. 13

7. Sew through the first beads you picked up in step 6. Pick up **either** an 11º or 15º, depending on which will fill the corner better **(fig. 7, a–b)**. Skip two 11ºs, pick up an 11º or 15º (whichever you picked up before), and sew through the next group of beads you picked up in step 6. Note: The 11ºs you skip will be below a group of four 11ºs along the edge. Always sew through the beads you picked up in step 6, not skipping any of them. Repeat, skipping and picking up one bead two times. Sew through two 11ºs, nine 15ºs, and three 11ºs **(c–e)**.

To attach to a bail

1. Pick up two 11ºs, and sew through the middle two 11ºs and the first 11º you picked up **(fig. 8)**. *Sew down through one 11º and up through two 11ºs* **(fig. 9)**. Repeat the section between the * until the bail is long enough to reach comfortably to the 11ºs on the back of the pendant. This will vary depending on the thickness of your cord, but 14 or 15 repetitions is a good start.

2. After the last repetition, sew through the center two beads if you picked up even numbers in step 6 or just the center bead if you picked up odd numbers **(fig. 10)**. Sew through one column. Sew through the two center 11ºs in the group of four 11ºs along the edge and down

the other column of beads. Continue through the 11º(s) in the back of the pendant and up the column again. Stop when you exit the last bead in the column **(fig. 11)**. Pick up six 15ºs, and check to make sure they will cover four 11ºs. Adjust the count if necessary. Sew up through a bead in the fifth row of the bail **(fig. 12, a)**. Sew down through the other bead in the same row **(b)**. Sew through the 15ºs. Sew up through the column that will force the 15ºs to be centered on the bail **(c)**. Weave the thread in, securing it with a couple of slip knots, and trim the excess thread.

To connect to a Trefoil Connector

(You must have a completed Trefoil Connector.) Pick up two 15ºs. Sew through an outside hole of one of the bricks in the Trefoil **(fig. 13, a–b)**. Pick up two 15ºs. Sew through the middle two 11ºs **(c–d)**. Sew through the beads again to strengthen the connection. Weave the thread in, securing it with a couple of slip knots. Trim the excess thread.

I have included this clasp for those of you who feel as though it's cheating to use a fabricated clasp. There is a certain satisfaction that comes with knowing you made every element in your piece of jewelry. If you do include this clasp in your design, keep in mind that it will add approximately 1¼" to the length of your necklace or bracelet.

materials per element
- **10** SuperDuos
- **2** 4mm heishi spacer beads
- **2** 3mm crystal pearls
- **1g** 11º seed beads
- **.5g** 15º seed beads
- **2** 4mm soldered jump rings
- Size D nylon thread

tools
- Size 12 needles
- Silicon thread conditioner
- Thread snips

⬭	SuperDuo
⬤	3mm crystal pearl
▮	11º seed bead
▯	15º seed bead
⬭⬭	4mm heishi bead

Make the ring

1. Stretch and condition 3' thread, and thread on a needle. Pick up an 11º seed bead and a SuperDuo ten times, and sew back through the first 11º and SuperDuo so the beads form a ring **(fig. 1)**. Pick up three 15º seed beads and sew through the free hole in the SuperDuo **(fig. 1, a–b)**. Pick up three 15ºs and sew through the same SuperDuo, an 11º, and another SuperDuo **(c–d)**. *Pick up three 15ºs, and sew through the free hole in the SuperDuo **(fig. 2, a–b)**. Pick up a 15º and sew through two 15ºs, a SuperDuo, an 11º, and a SuperDuo **(c–e)**. Repeat from the * seven times.

2. Continue through two 15ºs **(fig. 3, a)**. Pick up a 15º and sew through the SuperDuo. Pick up another 15º **(b–c)**. Sew through two 15ºs, a SuperDuo, an 11º, a SuperDuo, three 15ºs, a SuperDuo, and a 15º **(d–f)**.

3. Pick up an 11º. Sew through a 15º, a SuperDuo, and a 15º **(fig. 4)**. Repeat nine times. Continue through an 11º, pick up eight 15ºs and an 11º, and sew through a soldered jump ring and back through the 11º **(fig. 5, a–c)**. Pick up eight 15ºs. Sew through an 11º, a 15º, a Super-Duo, a 15º, and an 11º. Head toward the other strand connecting to the jump ring. Note that the strands of 15ºs are on the outsides of the 11ºs **(fig. 6)**.

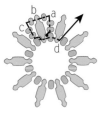

fig. 1

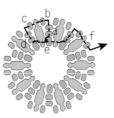

fig. 2

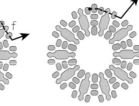

fig. 3

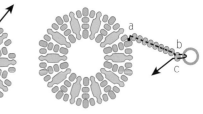

fig. 4   fig. 5

4. Sew through the 15°s, 11°, and jump ring. After the last (16th) 15°, pick up a 15° and sew through the nearest 15° on the edge of the ring **(fig. 7, a)**. Continue sewing around the edge. Stop after you sew through the 15° next to the ones connecting the jump ring to the toggle ring **(b)**. Pick up a 15° **(c)**. Sew through the 15°s, 11°, and jump ring one last time. Weave in the working thread and the tail, securing the threads with a couple of slip knots. Trim the excess thread.

Make the bar

5. Stretch and condition 4' thread, and thread a needle onto one end. Pick up four 11°s, and sew back through the first two, leaving an 8" tail **(fig. 8, a)**. Continue through the second two 11°s **(b)**. *Pick up two 11°s and sew back through the previous two 11°s **(fig, 9, a)**. Sew back through the two 11°s you just picked up **(b)**.* Repeat the section between the * once. Connect the two ends by sewing through each end once.

Technically, this elongated cube shape is called a rectangular parallelepiped or a rectangular prism. I'm just going to call it a rectangle.

6. Pick up two 11°s **(fig. 10, a)**. Position the beads so that they sit on top of two 11°s. Sew down through one 11° and up through the next 11° **(b–c)**. Pick up two 11°s **(fig. 11, a)**. Position the beads so they sit on top of two 11°s. Sew down through one 11° and up through the next two 11°s **(b–c)**. Repeat this step until you have a rectangle twelve beads long. Sew through each column to strengthen the stitching. After you have

sewn through all four columns, continue sewing until you bring your needle out through the sixth bead of the next column **(fig. 12)**.

7. Pick up an 11°, fourteen 15°s, and an 11°. Sew through a soldered jump ring and back through the 11° **(a–b)**. Pick up fourteen 15°s. Sew through the 11° next to the rectangle. Sew through two 11°s in the rectangle **(fig. 13)**. Note: it is very important that you start with the seventh 11° in the same column where you began this step. Go to the other column on this same side and sew through the seventh and sixth beads **(c)**. Sew through the 11°s and 15°s you picked up in this step and jump ring again. After you pass through the 11° next to the rectangle, try to sew through the bead that will allow you to have a thread leading from each of the four center beads into the connector **(fig. 14)**. Weave the thread and tail ends in a short distance, securing them with a couple of slip knots. Trim the excess thread.

8. Stretch and condition 18" thread, and thread a needle on one end. Pick up a heishi, a pearl, and a 15° **(fig. 15, a)**. Sew back through the pearl and the heishi **(b)**, leaving an 8" tail. Continue through the center of the rectangle, in the middle of the four columns **(c)**. Pick up a heishi, a pearl and a 15°. Sew back through the heishi and pearl. Sew back through the end beads and the rectangle again to reinforce. Sew the needle end through the rectangle to meet the tail and tie them together in a big knot. Thread a needle on the tail and pull both thread ends down into the rectangle. Trim the excess thread.

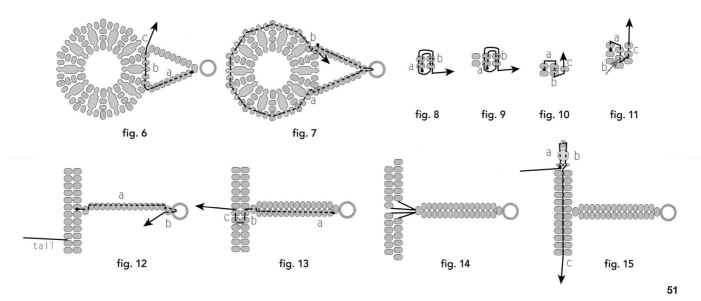

fig. 6   fig. 7   fig. 8   fig. 9   fig. 10   fig. 11

tail

fig. 12   fig. 13   fig. 14   fig. 15

...y the playful touch this graceful component brings to any design that features it—it's like including a tiny beaded act from Cirque de Soliel. To further personalize your design, consider using fire-polished beads in place of the 4mm crystal pearls, or a mix of both. Nine blocks will result in a 7" length of beadwork. Adding or subtracting a tile will alter the length by about ¾".

materials per 7" strap
- **9** tile beads, lentils, or brick beads
- **10** 4mm crystal bicones
- **18** 4mm crystal pearls
- **1g** 11º seed beads
- **5g** 15º seed beads
- **2** 4mm soldered jump rings
- Size D nylon thread

tools
- Size 10 and 12 needles
- Silicon thread conditioner
- Thread snips

1. Stretch and condition 6' thread for a bracelet (3' for an earring), and thread one end through a size 10 needle. Leaving a 10" tail, tie the other end to a jump ring with a lark's head knot (Basics).

2. Pick up an 11º seed bead, a 4mm bicone, an 11º, a 15º seed bead, an 11º, a tile, an 11º, three 15ºs, and an 11º.

3. Sew through the free hole in the tile **(fig. 1)**, and pick up an 11º and three 15ºs **(fig. 2, a–b)**. Sew through an 11º, a tile, an 11º, three 15ºs, an 11º, the other hole in the same tile, an 11º, and a 15º **(c–e)**. Sew back through an 11º, a tile, and an 11º **(fig. 3)**. Pick up a 15º, an 11º, a bicone, an 11º, a 15º, an 11º, a tile, an 11º, three 15ºs, and an 11º. Repeat this step until you have used all the tiles. You'll end by sewing through an 11º, a tile, and an 11º. Pick up a 15º, an 11º, a bicone, and an 11º, sew through a soldered jump ring, and then sew back through an 11º, a bicone, and an 11º.

If you don't want the extra dangle on an earring, don't sew through a jump ring at the end of step 3. Sew back through the bicone and the 11º, and then go to step 4.

4. Pick up two 15ºs, an 11º, a 15º, a 4mm pearl, a 15º, an 11º, and two 15ºs. Sew through the next 11º, bicone, and 11º **(fig. 4)**. Continue adding swags down one side of the bracelet. After you pass through the last 11º, bicone, and 11º, sew through the soldered jump ring. Sew back through the 11º, bicone, and 11º. Add a second series of swags along the other side of the bracelet. Pass through all the swags again to strengthen the stitching. You can keep track of which side you've done by always holding the tiles the same way. For example, always go from the top corner diagonally to the bottom corner **(photo)**. For the other set of swags, reverse directions.

5. Weave in the thread a short distance, securing it with a couple of slip knots. Trim the excess thread. Thread a needle on the tail and repeat.

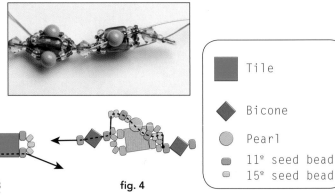

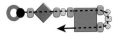
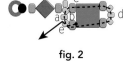

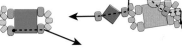

▪	Tile
◆	Bicone
●	Pearl
▪	11º seed bead
▫	15º seed bead

fig. 1   fig. 2   fig. 3   fig. 4

Titania is inclined to curve, which makes it very suitable for a necklace strap or a bracelet. This strap needs to have a fairly snug fit as a bracelet and looks best in a necklace when it comes from the back of the neck to approximately the collarbone.

materials per inch
- **3** two-hole lentils
- **26** 8º seed beads
- **2** 11º seed beads
- **17** 15º seed beads, color A
- **26** 15º seed beads, color B
- Size D nylon thread

other materials
- **3** 4mm soldered jump rings

tools
- Size 10 and 12 needles
- Silicon thread conditioner
- Thread snips

Allow 18–24 lentils, 8g 8º seed beads, 12–20 11º seed beads, and at least .5g A and 1g B 15º seed beads for a bracelet or a strap. You can make the strap whatever length you like, but the number of rows must always be a multiple of three, plus one.

	Two-hole lentil
	8º seed bead
	11º seed bead
	15º seed bead, A
	15º seed bead, B

1. Stretch and condition a comfortable length of thread, and thread a size 10 needle. Pick up two 8º seed beads, and sew back through the first one so that the beads sit next to each other **(fig. 1)**. Leave a 10" tail.

2. Pick up two 8ºs and sew down through one bead in the previous row **(fig. 2, a–b)**. Sew up through the other bead in the previous row **(c–d)**. Repeat this step until the strap is long enough, making sure that the total number of rows is a multiple of three, plus one (such as 15 +1). Allow an extra ¾" for the jump ring connections in your total length. After the last pair of 8ºs has been sewn on, sew through one of the pair and then the other to make them lie flat. Sew through the first one again **(fig. 3)**. Sew up through one column and down through the other to tighten the stitching.

  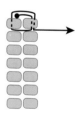

fig. 1   fig. 2   fig. 3

The best way to add thread is to weave the old thread into the 8ºs. Then prepare a new thread and tie the old thread and the new thread together. Hide the knot in the 8ºs. Weave back to where you left off and keep going. Leave the thread ends flapping in the breeze until you are completely done. You can trim them to about an inch or so. It is very untidy-looking, but you may need to know where those knots are at some point.

times **(fig. 3)**. Work your needle and thread out of the 11º across from the tail **(fig. 4)**.

4. Pick up an 8º, a 6º, an 8º, and an 11º three times, and then pick up an 8º, a 6º, and an 8º for a total of 15 beads. Sew through the 11º at the end of the previous square and the first 8º, 6º, and 8º **(fig. 5, a–b)**.

5. Repeat from step 2 until the beadwork is the desired length. End on a repeat of step 3.

6. Pick up two 11ºs **(fig. 6, a)**, and sew through a jump ring and back through three 11ºs **(b–c)**. Pick up an 11º, sew through an 11º and the jump ring **(fig. 7, a)**, and sew back through the 11º next to the jump ring and the 11º you just picked up **(b–c)**. Continue sewing through the 8ºs and 6ºs **(d–g)**. Sew through an 11º **(h)**, and sew through the 11º next to the jump ring. You will probably have to switch to a size 12 needle at this point. Sew through the jump ring and back through two 11ºs. Weave through some 8ºs and 6ºs in the last square, securing the thread with a couple of slip knots. Trim the excess thread.

7. Remove the stop bead and thread a needle on the tail. Repeat step 6. If you are making earrings and do not want a jump ring at both ends, just weave the tail in.

fig. 5

fig. 6

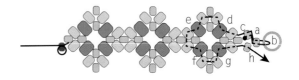

fig. 7

You'll enjoy the interplay between the roundness of the pearls and the tapered SuperDuos in this component. It may turn out to be a creative potato chip—you can't make just one because of how beautiful the tango is by itself. (Each section is approximately ½" long.)

materials (first element)
- **4** SuperDuos
- **4** 3mm crystal pearls
- **8** 11º seed beads
- **16** 15º seed beads

subsequent elements
- **4** SuperDuos
- **3** 3mm crystal pearls
- **8** 11ºs
- **16** 15ºs

other materials
- **2** 4mm soldered jump rings
- **2** 11ºs
- **12** 15ºs
- Size D nylon thread

tools
- Size 10 and 12 needles
- Silicon thread conditioner
- Thread snips

Once again, don't overlook the earring potential of the Right-Angle Tango—try a pair with one, two, or three sections. This is another element that could make a stunning wrap bracelet.

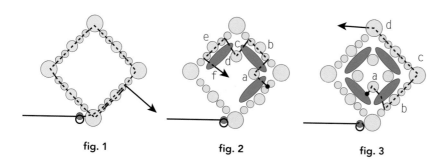

fig. 1   fig. 2   fig. 3

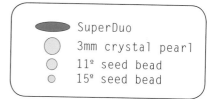

- ⬭ SuperDuo
- ◯ 3mm crystal pearl
- ◌ 11º seed bead
- ○ 15º seed bead

1. Stretch and condition 3' thread for an earring (8' for a bracelet), and thread a size 10 needle. String a stop bead and slide it 12" from the end. Pick up a 3mm pearl, and slide it to the stop bead.

2. Pick up two 15º seed beads, an 11º seed bead, two 15ºs, and a pearl three times times. Pick up an additional two 15ºs, 11º, and two 15ºs. Sew through the first pearl, two 15ºs, an 11º, and a 15º so the beads form a ring (**fig. 1**).

3. Pick up a SuperDuo, an 11º, and a SuperDuo, skip a 15º, a pearl, and 15º, and sew through a 15º, an 11º, and a 15º (**fig. 2, a–b**). Sew through the free hole in the second SuperDuo (**c**).

4. Pick up an 11º and a SuperDuo (**d**), skip a 15º, a pearl, and 15º, and sew through a 15º, an 11º, a 15º and the free hole in the SuperDuo (**e–f**). Repeat.

5. Pick up an 11º, and sew through the free hole in the SuperDuo, a 15º, and an 11º (**fig. 3, a–b**). Continue through the beads along the outside until you sew through the pearl across from the tail (**c–d**).

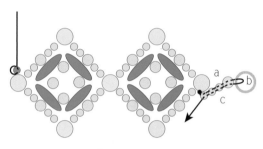

fig. 4

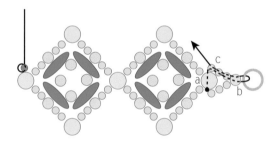

fig. 5

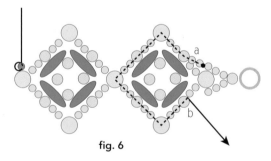

fig. 6

6. Repeat steps 2–4 until you have enough sections. If you are making a bracelet or a link, reinforce each link after you complete step 4 by sewing through all the beads along the outside edge once. This is not necessary if you are making earrings, although it can help to correct loose tension. Do not reinforce the first and last sections—you will reinforce those when you sew on the jump rings or weave in the threads.

7. To sew on the jump rings, switch to a size 12 needle. Pick up three 15°s and an 11°, and sew through a jump ring and back through the 11° and the 15°s **(fig. 4)**. Continue through the pearl, pick up three 15°s, and sew through the 11° and the jump ring **(fig. 5, a–b)**. Sew back through the 11° and the three 15°s that you just picked up **(c)**.

8. Pick up two 15°s, and sew through an 11° **(fig. 6, a)**. Continue sewing through the beads on the outside edge. Stop after you sew through the fourth 11° **(b)**. Pick up two 15°s, and sew through three 15°s, an 11°, and the jump ring. Sew back into the end section and secure the tail with a couple of slip knots. Trim the excess thread.

9. Remove the stop bead and thread. Repeat steps 6 and 7 if you want a jump ring at both ends, or just weave the tail into the end section, securing it with a couple of slip knots. Trim the excess threads.

projects

Crown Jewel *earrings*

Atlantic green colorway

materials
- **2** 12x8 crystal AB drops
- **6** purple iris SuperDuos, color A
- **3** transparent lilac Super Duos, color B
- **2** 6mm purple velvet bicones
- **2** 4mm light amethyst bicones
- **4** 3mm fancy spacers
- **2** 2.5mm round metal beads
- .25g frosted silver-lined 11º seed beads
- .25g purple iris 15º seed beads, color E
- .5g light amethyst ceylon 15ºs, color F
- **2** 5mm bead caps
- **2** 3-in. 22-gauge headpins
- Pair of earring wires
- Size D nylon thread

Atlantic green

- 12x8 gray-green crystal drops
- Blue luster SuperDuos
- Green luster SuperDuos
- 6mm erinite bicones
- 4mm Indian sapphire bicones
- Pewter-lined 11ºs
- Lime-lined crystal AB 15ºs
- Peridot-lined emerald 15ºs

tools
- Size 12 and 13 needles
- Silicon thread conditioner
- Thread snips
- Chainnose pliers
- Roundnose pliers

This pair of earrings has a jaw-dropping effect. They would be wonderful earrings for bridesmaids when made in wedding colors. But don't deny yourself the pleasure of wearing a pair for other occasions!

1. Make two Crown Jewel Drops, p. 40. Complete the wrapped loops (Basics).
2. Open the loops on the ear wires and hang one jewel from each earring wire. Close the loops.

Onion Dome *earrings*

A pair of these links is quite suitable for a couple of earrings. The somewhat open weave means that they're lighter than you might think. As a bonus, the way the berry beads catch light as the earrings move adds a subtle hint of sparkle.

1. Make two Onion Dome Links, p. 32. (Don't make the variation unless you want to eliminate the drops.)

2. To make the dangles, on each headpin string: a drop (point down), a bead cap, and a round spacer. (For the Mystery colorway, string two bead caps with a pearl between them.) Attach a dangle to each link with a wrapped loop.

3. Attach an earring wire to the other loop on each link.

materials
- 2 15x8 matte light siam glass drops
- 8 halo cardinal brick beads
- 8 red wine SuperDuos
- 20 honey beige berry beads
- 2 3mm round metal spacers
- 4 blackberry 3mm crystal pearls
- .25g root beer AB 11º seed beads
- .75g dark peach-lined 15º seed beads
- 2 9mm bead caps
- 2 2" headpins
- 4 4mm soldered jump rings
- Pair of earring wires
- Size D nylon thread

Mystery
- 9x6 brown iris glass drops
- Turquoise moondust brick beads
- Opaque olivine SuperDuos
- Black-lined crystal AB berry beads
- Petrol 4mm crystal pearls
- Petrol 3mm crystal pearls
- 2 2mm round metal spacers
- Blue iris 11º s
- Brown iris 15º s
- 5mm bead caps
- 4mm bead caps

tools
- Size 12 needles
- Silicon thread conditioner
- Thread snips

Mystery colorway

Festival *earrings*

Just putting on these earrings might make you feel ready for a party! If you want a lighter earring, substitute a 6mm crystal bicone for the drop because the swinging dangle adds to the festivities.

Woodland violets colorway

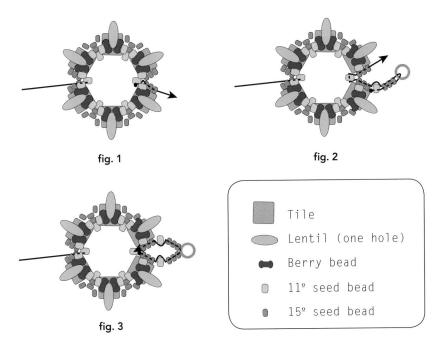

fig. 1

fig. 2

fig. 3

Tile

Lentil (one hole)

Berry bead

11º seed bead

15º seed bead

materials
- **2** 15x8 glass jet drops
- **12** jet tiles
- **12** jet marea lentils
- **24** crystal AB berry beads
- **.25g** jet 11º seed beads
- **.25g** transparent lime AB 15º seed beads
- **2** 9mm bead caps
- **2** 5mm bead caps
- **2** 2.5mm spacers
- **4** 4mm soldered jump rings
- **2** 2" decorative headpins
- Pair of earring wires
- Size D nylon thread

Woodland violets

- 12x8 faceted amethyst glass drops
- Tanzanite tiles
- Prairie green lentils
- Purple-lined crystal berry beads
- Erinite 4mm bicones
- Silver-lined amethyst AB 11ºs
- Peridot-lined emerald 15ºs

tools
- Size 12 needles
- Silicon thread conditioner
- Thread snips
- Roundnose pliers
- Chainnose pliers
- Flush cutters

1. Make a Festival link, p. 19.

2. After you sew through the 11º opposite the 11º with the tail, continue through three 15ºs **(fig. 1)**. *Pick up an 11º and three 15ºs. Sew through a soldered jump ring. Sew back through three 15ºs. Skip the 11º and sew through three 15ºs, an 11º, and three 15ºs **(fig. 2)**. Pick up an 11º and three 15ºs, and sew through the jump ring and back through three 15ºs. Skip the 11º and sew through the next three 15ºs. Sew through just the 12 15ºs again **(fig. 3)**. Weave in your thread, securing it with a couple of slip knots. Trim the excess thread.* Thread a needle on the tail and sew through three 15ºs. Repeat the section between the *.

3. Repeat steps 1 and 2 to make a second link.

4. String bead caps, beads, and drops on the headpins as desired, using the photos as a guide. Use wrapped loops to hang a dangle from a jump ring on each link. Use the free jump rings to hang the links from earring wires.

Sunburst
earrings

Radiant is the best word to describe these earrings—and they'll make you or whoever is graced with them look radiant as well.

Amber flame colorway

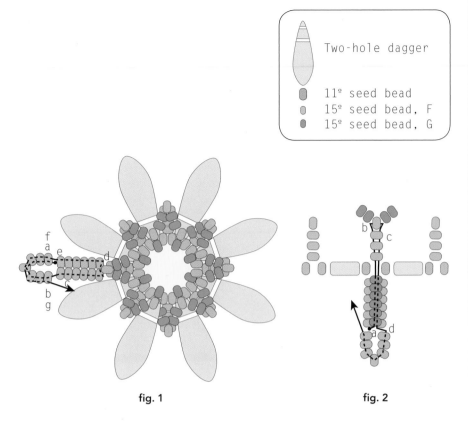

Two-hole dagger

●	11º seed bead
○	15º seed bead, F
●	15º seed bead, G

fig. 1

fig. 2

materials
- **2** 12mm crystal AB rivolis
- **16** iris-lustered cobalt two-hole daggers
- **2** 4mm light turquoise bicone crystals
- .25g 11º blue iris seed beads
- 1g trans-rainbow aquamarine 15º seed beads (color F when noted)
- 1g amethyst-lined crystal 15º s (color G when noted)
- **2** 4mm soldered jump rings
- Pair of earring wires
- Size D nylon thread
- **2** SS20 Bermuda blue flat-back crystals (optional)
- Epoxy clay (optional)
- Antique silver mica powder (optional)

Amber flame

- 12mm topaz rivoli crystals
- Luster iris topaz two-hole daggers
- 4mm topaz AB bicone crystals
- Opaque brown 11º s
- Ivory ceylon 15º s (color F)
- Silver-lined topaz 15º s (color G)
- SS20 light Colorado topaz flat-back crystals
- Bronze mica powder

tools
- Size 12 and 13 needles
- Silicon thread conditioner
- Thread snips
- Small craft paintbrush (optional)
- Toothpick with a small blob of wax on one tip or tweezers (optional)
- Pencil with an eraser (optional)

These earrings feature a variation on the bar. If you do not want to use jump rings, follow the instructions given for the Amber flame colorway.

1. Make two 8-pointed Sunbursts, p. 8. Next, start with step 2 of the Herringbone Bar Connector, p. 45. For the main colorway, follow the instruction for the bar as written. For the Amber flame colorway, make a bar six beads long. Next, pick up seven F 15º s **(fig. 1, a–b)**, and sew down one column and up the other **(c–e)**. Continue through the seven beads in the loop **(f–g)**.

2. Pick up seven G 15º s, and sew through four F 15º s, ending with a point bead **(fig. 2, a–b)**. Sew back through three F 15º s and seven G 15º s, and continue through the seven loop 15º s, starting with the side not connected to the Gs **(c–d)**. Weave the thread in a short distance and trim the excess. Use the jump rings or the loops to hang the Sunbursts from the earring wires.

3. **Optional epoxy clay backing:** Include this if you don't like the bare back of the rivoli showing (Basics).

71

Origami *earrings*

Do you remember making folded paper fortune-tellers in school? The shape is actually called the salt-cellar. No matter what you called it, here it is, all grown-up, in this double-sided earring.

Serenity colorway

1. Stretch and condition 5' thread, and thread on a needle. Follow steps 1–10 of Origami Link, p. 20. Work your needle through a pearl. *Pick up a 15º seed bead, three 11º seed beads, and a 15º. Sew through the next pearl.* Make sure that these beads are closer to the base of the triangle than the point **(fig. 1)**. Repeat the section between * three times, and sew through a 15º and three 11ºs with no triangle.

2. Refer to the Origami Link to make a second Origami backing up to the first one: Use the pearls already in place rather than picking up new ones. Work your thread through the pearl opposite the tail. *Pick up two 15ºs, three 11ºs, and two 15ºs. Sew through the next pearl* **(fig. 2, a–b)**. Make sure these beads rest on the two previous sets of beads connecting the pearls. Repeat the section between the * three times. Continue through two 15ºs **(c–d)**.

3. Pick up three 15ºs and an 11º **(fig. 3, a–b)**. Sew through a soldered jump ring, and sew through an 11º, five 15ºs, a pearl, and two 15ºs **(c–d)**. Pick up three 15ºs, and sew through the 11º and the jump ring. Sew back through the 11º, five 15º, pearl, and two 15ºs. Set aside the thread for now and thread a needle onto the tail.

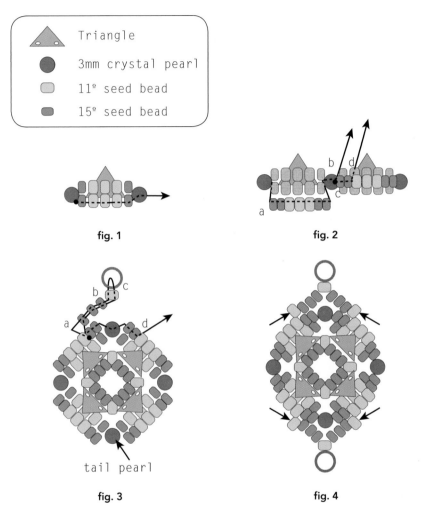

fig. 1

fig. 2

tail pearl

fig. 3

fig. 4

Legend:
- ▲ Triangle
- ● 3mm crystal pearl
- ▢ 11º seed bead
- ▢ 15º seed bead

materials

- **2** sand opal 13x6.5 briolettes
- **2** bronze 2x4mm bicone crystals
- **8** opaque champagne luster triangles
- **8** bronze 3mm crystal pearls
- **.5g** antique bronze 11º seed beads
- **.25g** brown iris 15º seed beads
- **4** antique brass 4mm soldered jump rings
- **2** 4x6 antique brass oval jump rings
- **2** 4mm brass bead caps
- **2** 2mm antique brass spacers
- **2** 2" 24-gauge antique brass ball headpins
- Pair of antique brass earring wires
- Size D nylon thread

Serenity

- 15x9 light sapphire glass drops
- Sapphire triangles
- Light blue 3mm crystal pearls
- Pewter-lined 11ºs
- Amethyst-lined crystal AB 15ºs

other materials

- **2** 9mm silver bead caps
- **2** 2mm spacers

tools

- Size 10 and 12 needles
- Silicon thread conditioner
- Thread snips

4. Repeat step 4 to attach a second jump ring. Secure each thread with a couple of slip knots, and trim the excess thread.

If the earring doesn't seem to hang right, follow the thread path shown in figure 4, picking up 15ºs indicated by the arrows. You can also use 11ºs; just use all the same size.

5. Main colorway: On a headpin, string a bicone, a bead cap, and a spacer. Use a wrapped loop to connect to a jump ring. Repeat with another headpin and the other Origami element. Use the oval jump rings to hang briolettes from the origamis. Attach the earring wires to the free jump rings. **Serenity colorway:** On each headpin, string a drop (point down), a bead cap, and a spacer. Use wrapped loops to hand a dangle from each origami link. Attach the earring wires to the free jump ring.

Byzantine *bracelet*

I recommend you use either a heavy-weight chain or double a medium-weight chain and attach a hefty clasp to help weight the bracelet properly. It will look better if the fit is reasonably snug, which will also help keep it in position on your wrist.

Joyful noise colorway

1. Make one Lattice Bezel, p. 22, and two Caned elements, p. 18. Weave the thread in, securing it with a couple of slip knots. Trim the excess thread. Avoid the pairs of 11º seed beads on the outside of the triangles in the Lattice and the pairs of 11ºs on the underside of the bricks in the Caned elements. You will be stringing through these, and it will not help to have these beads clogged up with extra thread.

2. Cut the beading wire into two equal pieces. Crimp a wire on each loop of the two-loop side of a 2-to-1 connector (Basics).

3. On one wire, string: a 4mm bicone, a heishi, a 4mm pearl, a heishi, a 6mm bicone, an 11º, and a 15º seed bead. Take one of the Caned components and use a size 10 needle to make sure that two pairs of 11ºs opposite each other have enough room for the wire

a

b

(photo a). Pass the wire through one of these. String a 15º, an 11º, a 6mm bicone, a heishi, a 4mm pearl, a heishi, a 6mm bicone, an 11º, and a 15º. Check the holes in two pairs of 11ºs opposite each other in the Lattice (photo b). String through one of these pairs. Make sure the components face the same way. String a 15º, an 11º, a 6mm bicone, a heishi, a 4mm pearl, a heishi, a 6mm bicone, an 11º, and a 15º. Check the holes in two pairs of 11ºs opposite each other in the second Caned component and string through one of these pairs. Again, make sure all the components are facing the same way. String a 15º, an 11º, a 6mm bicone, a heishi, a 4mm pearl, a heishi, and a 4mm bicone. Crimp the wire to one of the loops on the second side of the other connector.

Before you crimp, check to see how the bracelet lies. It is not unusual for the bracelet to want to twist or for the connector to flip in the wrong direction. If this is the case, remove the wire guardian from the connector and try again. Or, you can pull the wire out of the guardian and try passing it through the guardian from the other side.

4. Repeat step 3 with the second cable. It is even more important that you check how the bracelet lies when you crimp this wire after you're done stringing the beads. Almost certainly, you will have to reposition the guardian or the wire at least once.

5. If you are using a heavy-weight chain, cut it into two equal pieces, ideally with an odd number of links. If you are using a medium-weight chain, cut it into four equal pieces with an odd number of links in each piece of chain. Use an oval jump ring to connect a heavy-weight piece of chain to each connector or a 6mm jump ring to connect two pieces of medium-weight chain to each connector. Use another jump ring to connect the ring part of the toggle to the chain(s) on one connector. Connect the soldered jump ring to the other end of chain with one of the oval rings. Connect the bar part of the toggle to the soldered ring with the second oval jump ring. Joyful noise colorway: Use the second 6mm jump ring to connect the bar to the chains on the second connector.

materials
lattice component (1)
- 14mm golden shadow crystal ring
- 6 opaque luster champagne two-hole triangles
- 6 3mm bronze crystal pearls
- .5g bronze 11º seed beads
- .5g brown iris 15º seed beads

caned components (2)
- 2 14mm tabac crystal squares
- 8 beige brown iris bricks
- 16 3mm antique brass crystal pearls
- .75g matte metallic dark raspberry 11ºs
- .5g gold-lined crystal AB 15ºs

other materials
- 12 6mm crystal honey bicones
- 8 4mm antique brass crystal pearls
- 4 4mm crystal honey bicones
- 16 3mm heishi beads
- 12 bronze 11ºs
- 12 brown iris 15ºs
- 2 2-to-1 connector bars
- 2" heavy chain
- 4 2x2 crimp tubes, fine wire guardians, and 3mm crimp covers
- 4mm soldered jump ring
- 5 20-gauge oval jump rings
- 16" .014 beading cable
- Toggle clasp set
- Size D nylon thread

Joyful noise

- 14mm rose rivoli
- 14mm vitrail light crystal squares
- 6mm light turquoise bicones
- 4mm blackberry crystal pearls
- 4mm light turquoise bicones
- 3mm rose pearls
- 3mm blackberry crystal pearls
- 3mm heishi beads
- Beige halo light pink bricks
- Halo amethyst two-hole triangles
- Silver-lined extra-dark amethyst 11ºs
- Black-lined crystal AB 15ºs
- Peridot-lined emerald 15ºs

tools
- Size 10 and 12 needles
- Silicon thread conditioner
- Thread snips
- Crimping pliers
- Macro crimper or chainnose pliers
- Wire cutters

Quaternity *bracelet*

This bracelet has an elusive quality. The finished length of the beadwork is 7", plus your clasp. Adding or subtracting beaded beads adjusts the length about ½" (more or fewer bezels alter the length by about ¾"). You can also adjust the length by using a few extra jump rings to connect the clasp.

Imperial splendor colorway

1. Make Quatrefoil Bezels, p. 28. Do not bundle your thread; instead, secure it in the center square made up of the four sets of three 15⁰s. If you are not sure what the final length needs to be, just make three or four bezels to start. Make more as needed and connect them as you go.

2. Stretch and condition approximately 3' of thread, and thread a size 12 needle. String a stop bead and slide it 8" from the tail.

3. Pick up a pearl and an 11⁰ seed bead, and sew through a soldered jump ring and back through the

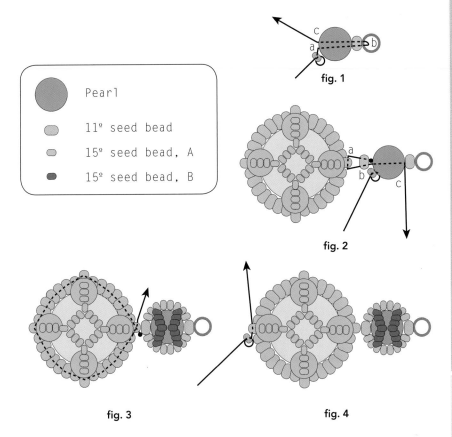

fig. 1

fig. 2

fig. 3

fig. 4

materials
quatrefoil bezels (6)
- **6** 12mm crystal rivolis
- **48** luster topaz/pink two-hole lentils
- **3g** amethyst gold luster 11º seed beads
- **1g** silver-lined champagne 15º seed beads

beaded beads (7)
- **7** 6mm blackberry crystal pearls
- **14** amethyst gold luster 11ºs
- **.75g** grape mist 15ºs, color A
- **.75g** silver-lined champagne 15ºs, color B

other materials
- **2** 4mm soldered jump ring
- **2** small oval jump rings
- Toggle clasp
- Size D nylon thread

Imperial splendor

- 12mm aquamarine rivolis
- 6mm petrol crystal pearls
- Blue iris two-hole lentils
- Silver-lined aquamarine AB 11ºs
- Silver-lined peridot 15ºs
- Silver-lined aquamarine 15ºs

tools
- Size 10 and 12 needles
- Silicon thread conditioner
- Thread snips
- Chainnose pliers

beads **(fig, 1, a–c)**. Pick up an 11º, and sew through a "popped" bead sandwiched between two lentils **(fig. 2, a)**. Sew back through the 11º and the pearl **(fig. 2, b–c)**.

4. Follow steps 2 and 3 of the Beaded Bead, p. 37. Then sew through an additional two color A 15º seed beads, the pearl, and an 11º. Reinforce the stitching as directed around the jump ring. When you sew through the 11º in the Quatrefoil, continue around the 11ºs circling the rivoli **(fig. 3)**. Finish the Beaded Bead. Secure the thread and tail inside the beaded bead, and trim the excess threads.

5. Stretch and condition another 3' of thread. String on a stop bead, leaving an 8" tail. Sew through the 11º sandwiched between two lentils **(fig. 4)**. Begin repeating from step 2 of the bracelet instructions

to connect a second Quatrefoil. When you reinforce the stitching around the rivoli, only reinforce it around the one that is already part of the bracelet, not the one you are just now connecting.

6. Repeat step 5 until all the Quatrefoils are connected to each other with Beaded Beads. Start a new thread as described in step 5 for the last beaded bead at the end of the bracelet. Pick up an 11º, a pearl, and an 11º, and sew through a soldered jump ring, an 11º, and a pearl. Begin repeating the Beaded Bead's instructions from step 2. Sew around the outside edge of the last Quatrefoil when you reinforce the stitching connecting the jump ring.

7. Connect the clasp with the oval jump rings.

Origami *bracelet*

Mango parfait colorway

When seen in a series, Origami Links have strikingly clean, modern lines. Yet the bracelet still will evoke tradition and childhood when you tell people its name. Consider making one for a childhood friend to let her know how much she's meant to you over the years. Each Origami Link is approximately ½" long.

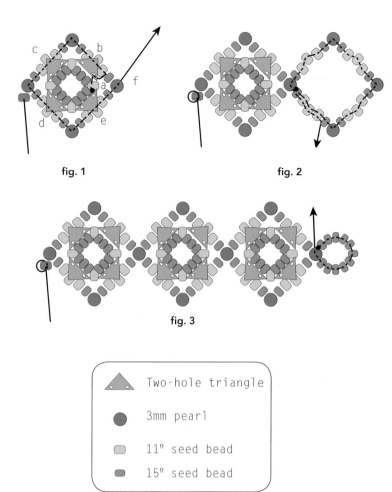

fig. 1

fig. 2

fig. 3

Two-hole triangle

3mm pearl

11º seed bead

15º seed bead

materials
- **44** silver two-hole triangle beads
- **34** 3mm dark gray crystal pearls
- 3g pewter-lined crystal 11º seed beads
- .75g transparent black diamond AB 15º seed beads
- **2** 4mm soldered jump rings
- **2** 20-gauge small oval jump rings
- Toggle clasp
- Size D thread

Mango parfait

- Maple orange two-hole triangle beads
- 3mm light peach crystal pearls
- Silver-lined orange AB 11ºs
- Peach-lined crystal AB 15ºs

tools
- Size 10 and 12 needles
- Silicon thread conditioner
- Thread snips
- Chainnose pliers

1. Stretch and condition 8' thread, and string a stop bead, leaving an 8" tail. Follow steps 2–9 of the Origami Link, p. 20. Sew through an 11º and a triangle **(fig. 1, a)**. Starting with three 11º seed beads, sew around the outside of the link, ending when you sew through the pearl opposite the stop bead **(b–f)**.

2. Pick up a 15º seed bead, three 11ºs, a 15º, and a pearl three times, pick up an additional 15º, three 11ºs, and 15º, and sew through the end pearl, a 15º, and three 11ºs so that the beads form a ring **(fig. 2)**. Follow steps 3–9 of the Origami Link, and then sew through an 11º and a triangle. Starting with three 11ºs, sew around the outside of the link, ending when you sew through the pearl opposite the stop bead.

Repeat this step (step 2 of the bracelet) as many times as necessary. You will have 11 Origami Links total.

3. To make a loop finish: Pick up eleven 15ºs and sew back through the pearl **(fig. 3)**. Sew through the 15ºs a few more times to strengthen the stitching, switching to a size 12 needle if necessary. Weave in the thread a short distance, securing it with a couple of slip knots. Trim the excess thread. Remove the stop bead and thread a needle on the tail. Sew another loop onto the tail end. Weave in and secure the thread. Trim the excess. Use one oval jump ring to connect the ring part of the toggle to one loop. Connect the soldered jump ring to the other loop with one of the oval

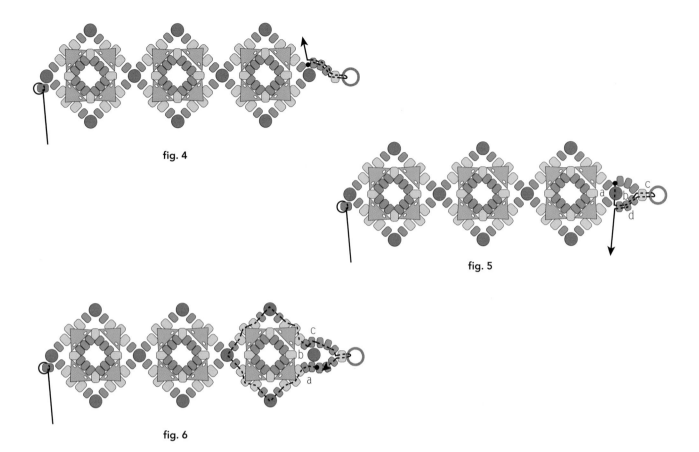

fig. 4

fig. 5

fig. 6

jump rings. Connect the bar part to the soldered jump ring with the last oval jump ring.

4. To finish with a jump ring: Pick up three 15ºs and an 11º. Sew through a soldered jump ring and back through the 11º, three 15ºs **(fig. 4)**. Sew through the pearl and pick up three 15ºs **(fig. 5, a–b)**. Sew through the 11º and the jump ring **(c)**. Sew back through the 11º and the three 15ºs you just picked up **(c)**. Pick up a 15º **(fig. 6, a)**. Sew through a 15º, three 11ºs, and the rest of the beads in the outside ring of the last

Origami Link, ending when you sew through the 15º on the other side of the end pearl **(b)**. Pick up a 15º **(c)**. Sew through the jump ring and the beads connecting it to the origami figure again. Weave the thread into the figure a short distance, securing it with a couple of slip knots. Trim the excess thread. Remove the stop bead and thread a needle onto the tail. Sew another soldered jump ring on the tail end as described in this step. Use oval jump rings to connect the clasp.

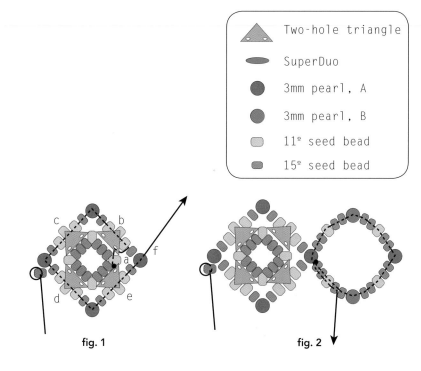

Legend:
- Two-hole triangle
- SuperDuo
- 3mm pearl, A
- 3mm pearl, B
- 11º seed bead
- 15º seed bead

fig. 1   fig. 2

materials
- **24** light green metallic suede two-hole triangles
- **20** pastel petrol SuperDuos
- **24** 3mm petrol crystal pearls, color A
- **10** 3mm light blue crystal pearls, color B
- 2.5g silver-lined aqua 11º seed beads
- 1.5g silver-lined blue zircon 15º seed beads
- **2** 4mm soldered jump rings
- **2** small oval jump rings
- Clasp set
- Size D nylon thread

English garden

- Purple iris two-hole triangles
- Purple luster SuperDuos
- 3mm light peach crystal pearls
- 3mm mauve crystal pearls
- Rosaline AB 11º s
- Peridot-lined emerald 15º s

tools
- Size 10 and 12 needles
- Silicon thread conditioner
- Thread snips
- Chainnose pliers

Makes a bracelet approximately 6½" long, plus clasp. Adding or subtracting either kind of link affects the overall length by approximately ½".

1. Stretch and condition 8' thread, and string a stop bead, leaving an 8" tail. Follow steps 2–9 of the Origami Link, p. 20. Use only color A crystal pearls. Sew through an 11º and a triangle **(fig. 1, a)**. Starting with three 11º s, sew around the outside of the link, ending when you sew through the pearl opposite the stop bead **(b–e)**.

2. Pick up two 15º s, an 11º, two 15º s, a color B crystal pearl, two 15º s, an 11º, two 15º s, a color A crystal pearl, two 15º s, an 11º, two 15º s, a color B crystal pearl, two 15º s, an 11º, and two 15º s, and sew through the pearl at the end of the origami, two 15º s, an 11º, and a 15º so the beads form a loop **(fig. 2)**.

3. Follow steps 3–5 of the Right-Angle Tango, p. 57. Sew completely around the outside of the link to strengthen it and tighten the tension. Sew through the end pearl.

4. Follow step 2 of the Origami Bracelet, p. 79. After you have completed the entire origami figure, sew completely around the outside edge to reinforce the stitching and tighten the tension.

5. Repeat steps 2–4 until you have six Origami Links and five Right-Angle Tangos. Sew the soldered jump rings on as directed and finish off the bracelet as described in step 4 of the Origami Bracelet.

Sun-Kissed *wrist*

Otherworlds colorway

The Sunburst element shines as a focal point in a bracelet. Beautifully set off by Coffee Bean Links, it says, "Wake up and admire me!" in more than one way.

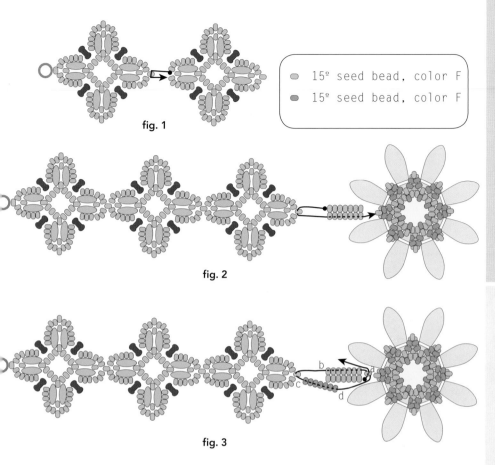

fig. 1

○ 15° seed bead, color F
● 15° seed bead, color F

fig. 2

fig. 3

materials

- 12mm jet rivoli
- **8** opaque red Picasso two-hole daggers
- **48** jet two-hole lentils
- **24** jet-lined crystal AB berry beads
- 1.75g jet 11° seed beads
- 2g black diamond AB 15° seed beads, color F
- **.25g** jet 15°s, color G
- **2** 4mm soldered jump rings
- **2** small 20-gauge oval jump rings
- Clasp set
- Size D thread

Otherworlds

- Light amethyst 12mm rivoli
- Tanzanite two-hole daggers
- Opaque lustered topaz two-hole lentils
- Transparent gray lustered berry beads
- Milky light amethyst 11°s
- Peridot-lined emerald 15°s, color F
- Silver-lined light amethyst 15°s, color G

tools

- Size 12 and 13 needles
- Thread snips

These instructions work into a bracelet about 7¼" long. To make a shorter bracelet, only connect two Coffee Bean links for each side. Adjust the fit by connecting jump rings to make a mini-chain. Also, a large, hefty yet decorative clasp is a clever way to increase the overall length (and a good way to keep the Sunburst where it belongs).

1. Make a Coffee Bean link, p. 30, with a jump ring at one point. Make a second Coffee Bean Link. Connect this link to the first one at the 11° seed bead opposite the jump ring. This means that instead of picking up an 11°, you will sew through one on the first Bean (**fig. 1**). Make a third link in the same way as the second. Make a second strap with three Coffee Bean Links.

2. Make an 8-point Sunburst, p. 8. Next, follow step 2 of the Herringbone Bar Connector, p. 45, only make the bar seven beads tall. After you finish the bar, sew through the 11° at the end of one strap. Sew down through all the beads in the bar's other column (**fig. 2**). Pick up a color F 15° seed bead, and sew up the other column (**fig. 3, a–b**). Sew through the 11°. Pick up seven color G 15° seed beads (**c–d**). Sew back through the the lone F (**a**) and back through the Gs. (If you want to omit the accent Gs, simply sew up and down through the columns and through the 11° a few times to reinforce.) Refer to fig. 7b of the Herringbone Bar Connector to weave to the opposite side of the Sunburst. Attach the other strap in the same way.

3. Use oval jump rings to connect the clasp.

Double
Diamonds
bracelet

Harvest gold colorway

No doubt you immediately saw how easily the Diamond Deluxe Strap can be made into a bracelet. Double the impact by doubling the width of the bracelet. The regular diamonds are reminiscent of embroidered smocking. Adding or subtracting a diamond will adjust the length by ½".

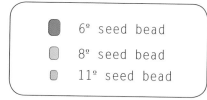

fig. 1

I recommend you use three-strand bars or clasps because the two-strand ones tend to have loops that are too close together. You need loops at least ½" apart. I like to put that spare middle loop to good use and embellish it with a little dangle.

Single-wide version

1. Stretch and condition 5' thread. Following the Diamond Deluxe Strap instructions, p. 55, make a strap 13 squares long. Sew on jump rings as directed. Use oval jump rings to connect the clasp.

Double-wide version

1. Stretch and condition 5' thread. Make one strap as directed in the single-wide version. Sew the jump rings onto the ends as directed. Stretch and condition 5' thread. String on a stop bead, leaving a 12" tail.

2. Pick up an 11º seed bead, an 8º seed bead, a 6º seed bead, and an 8º three times. Sew through an 11º on the side of the finished strap, heading toward the nearest jump ring **(fig. 1)**. Pick up an 8º, a 6º, and an 8º. Starting with the 11º next to the stop bead, sew through an 11º,

materials
single-wide version
- 4g opaque cobalt AB 6º seed beads
- 1.25g baby blue Ceylon 8º seed beads
- 1.25g pewter-lined crystal 11º seed beads
- **2** 4mm soldered jump rings
- **2** 20-gauge small oval jump rings
- Toggle clasp
- Size D nylon thread

Harvest gold
- Silver-lined topaz AB 6ºs
- Silver-lined dark gold AB 8ºs
- Silver-lined chartreuse 11ºs

double-wide version
- 8g opaque black 6ºs
- 3g silver-lined dark gold AB 8ºs
- 2.25g silver-lined chartreuse 11ºs
- **4** 4mm soldered jump rings
- **4** small 20-gauge oval jump rings
- Three-strand box clasp

optional dangle
- 6mm jet bicone
- 4mm silver shade bicone
- 1.5mm round spacer
- 5mm bead cap
- 4mm bead cap
- 22-gauge headpin

tools
- Size 12 and 13 needles
- Thread snips

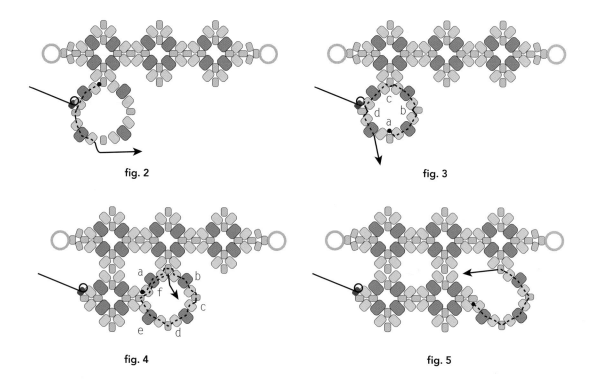

fig. 2

fig. 3

fig. 4

fig. 5

an 8º, a 6º, and an 8º (**fig. 2**). Skip an 11º and sew through an 8º, a 6º, and an 8º. Repeat twice (**fig. 3, a–c**). Skip an 11º and sew through an 8º and a 6º (**d**). Pick up an 11º and sew through a 6º. Repeat three times. Work your needle through the 11º across from the stop bead.

3. Pick up an 8º, a 6º, and an 8º, and sew through the next side 11º on the original strand (**fig. 4, a**). Pick up an 8º, a 6º, an 8º, and an 11º twice (**b–d**). Pick up an additional 8º, a 6º, and an 8º (**e**). Sew through an 11º, an 8º, a 6º and an 8º (**f**). Skip an 11º and sew through an 8º, a 6º, and an 8º. Repeat twice. Skip an 11º and sew through an 8º and a 6º. Pick up an 11º, and sew through a 6º. Repeat three times. Work your needle through the 11º at the end opposite the stop bead.

4. Pick up an 8º, a 6º, an 8º, and an 11º two times. Pick up an additional 8º, 6º, and 8º. Sew through the next side 11º, heading toward the stop bead (**fig. 5**). Pick up an 8º, a 6º, and an 8º, and sew through an 11º, an 8º, a 6º, and an 8º. Skip an 11º and sew through an 8º, a 6º, and an 8º. Repeat twice. Skip an 11º and sew through an 8º and a 6º. Pick up an 11º and sew through a 6º. Repeat three times. Work your needle through the 11º at the end opposite the stop bead.

5. Repeat steps 3 and 4 until you have completed the second half of the band. Sew on the jump rings as described in step 6 of the Diamond Deluxe Strap.

6. On the headpin, stack a 6mm bicone, a 5mm bead cap, a 4mm bicone, a 4mm bead cap, and the spacer. Make a wrapped loop to attach the headpin to the center loop of the female part of the box clasp. Do not attach it to the little clip that snaps inside the box. Attach the bracelet to the outer rings on the clasp with the oval jump rings.

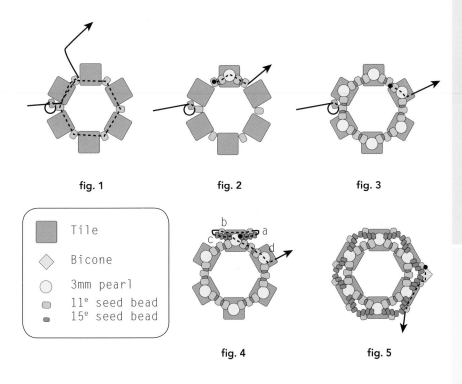

fig. 1   fig. 2   fig. 3

Tile

Bicone

3mm pearl

11º seed bead
15º seed bead

fig. 4   fig. 5

tiles. Repeat five times. These new 11ºs go behind the ones already in place. Weave in the tail through the 11ºs and tiles, securing it with a couple of slip knots. Trim the excess tail thread.

4. Using the original needle, pick up four 15ºs and an 11º. Sew through the free hole in a tile **(fig. 4, a–b)**. Pick up an 11º and four 15ºs. Sew through a pearl, an 11º, a 15º, an 11º, a 15º, an 11º, and a pearl **(c–d)**. Repeat this step five times. After you sew through the last pearl, continue through four 15ºs, an 11º, a tile, and a second 11º. Pick up a bicone, and sew through an 11º, a tile, and an 11º **(fig. 5)**. Sew in five more bicones in this manner.

5. Continue through the first bicone. Sew the soldered jump rings onto two bicones opposite each other as in step 5 of the Jewel-Encased Ring, p. 11 (refer to fig. 9 for jump ring placement). Weave in the thread a short distance,

securing it with a couple of slip knots. Trim the excess thread.

6. Follow step 1–4 of the Right-Angle Tango strap, p. 57. Sew the section to one of the jump rings on the ring as in step 6 of the Right-Angle Tango. Set this needle aside, and repeat this step to connect a second Right-Angle Tango section to the other soldered jump ring. Refer to step 5 of the Right-Angle Tango to sew additional sections. I recommend that you switch from side to side to make it easier to keep the ring centered. Sew a jump ring to each end of the Right-Angle Tango section as in step 6. Connect the ring part of the toggle with one of the oval jump rings. Connect the fifth soldered jump ring to the other end of the bracelet with an oval jump ring. Connect the bar part of the toggle to the soldered jump ring with the last oval jump ring.

materials
- **6** Siam tile beads
- **24** Siam ruby SuperDuos
- **6** dark red coral 4mm bicones
- **26** 3mm Bordeaux crystal pearls
- **1g** opaque red luster 11º seed beads
- **1g** semi-matte silver-lined light Siam 15º seed beads
- **5** 4mm soldered jump rings
- **3** 20-gauge small oval jump rings
- **Toggle clasp set**
- **Size D** nylon thread

Deep forest

- Twilight teal tiles
- Green iris SuperDuos
- Erinite 4mm bicones
- 3mm light green crystal pearls
- Silver-lined olive AB 11ºs
- Peridot-lined emerald 15ºs

Regal opulence

- Black currant tiles
- Opaque dark orchid SuperDuos
- Provence lavender 4mm bicones
- 3mm dark lapis crystal pearls
- Cobalt-lined sapphire AB 11ºs
- Silver-lined light grape 15ºs

tools
- Size 12 and 13 needles
- Thread snips
- Chainnose pliers
- Roundnose pliers

Inanna's bounty colorway

Ancient
Echoes
necklace

Truly, the adage "Less is more" is demonstrated completely in this extraordinary necklace. Only four components are featured in it, which allows each intricate handwoven jewel to stand out at the same time it complements the others.

Some people are bothered by the feel of bicones around their necks. If necessary, substitute round beads of the same size (crystal, glass, or even stone) for the three bicone sizes listed in the additional materials section.

a

Makes a necklace about 16¾" long, plus the clasp. The pendant hangs about 1¾".

If you have difficulty getting the beading wire to pass through the bricks, pass a size 10 needle through the hole to make a space for the wire.

1. Make two Turban elements, p. 14. Weave the thread ends in, avoiding the pairs of 11º seed beads on the bottom edge of the crystal rings.

2. Make two Temple elements, p. 16. Weave the thread ends in, avoiding the pairs of 11ºs along the bottom outside edge of the bricks.

3. Make a Trefoil Connector, p. 38.

4. Make a Royal Bezel Pendant, p. 47. Connect it to the Trefoil Connector as described on p. 49. Weave in the threads.

5. Cut a piece of beading wire to the specified length or work directly on your roll: String a crimp bead, three 3mm pearls, a 3mm spacer, a 4mm bicone, a 3mm spacer, and three 3mm pearls.

6. String a 3mm spacer, a 6mm bicone, a 3mm spacer, a 4mm pearl, a heishi, an 8mm bicone, a heishi, and a 4mm pearl. Repeat this step twice.

7. String a 3mm spacer, a 3mm pearl, and two 11º seed beads, and string through a Turban component **(photo a)**. Next, string a brown iris 11º, a 3mm pearl, a 3mm spacer, and a 4mm pearl.

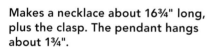

materials
turbans (2)
- **2** 14mm tabac crystal square rings
- **8** brown iris beige bricks
- **16** 3mm crystal honey bicones
- **8** 3mm bronze crystal pearls
- **1g** brown iris 11º seed beads
- **1g** gold-lined crystal AB 15º seed beads

temples (2)
- **2** 14mm tabac crystal square rings
- **8** brown iris beige bricks
- **8** 3mm antique brass crystal pearls, color A
- **8** 3mm bronze crystal pearls, color B
- **1g** matte metallic brown 11ºs
- **1g** gold-lined crystal AB 15ºs

trefoil connector (1)
- **3** brown iris beige bricks
- **3** 3mm antique brass crystal pearls, color P
- **3** 3mm bronze crystal pearls, color C
- **.5** brown iris 11ºs
- **.5g** gold-lined crystal AB 15ºs, color F
- **.25g** brown iris 15ºs, color G

royal bezel pendant (1)
- **25mm** yellow quartz donut
- **4** brown iris beige bricks
- **12** gold-lined berry beads
- **8** 3mm bronze crystal pearls
- **.75g** brown iris 11ºs
- **1.25g** gold-lined crystal AB 15ºs

(Materials continued on p. 98)

tools
- Size 10 and 12 needles
- Silicon thread conditioner
- Thread snips
- Flush cutters
- Crimp tool
- Macro-crimper or chainnose pliers for closing crimp covers

additional materials
- **10** 8mm crystal honey bicones
- **6** 6mm crystal honey bicones
- **20** 4mm antique brass crystal pearls
- **2** 4mm crystal honey bicones
- **22** 3mm deep brown crystal pearls
- **26** fancy 3mm spacers
- **20** 3mm heishi spacers
- **12** brown iris 11ºs
- **21** gold-lined crystal AB 15ºs
- **2** 2x2 crimp beads
- **2** small wire guardians
- **2** 3mm crimp covers
- 20" .014 beading wire
- Clasp set
- Size D nylon thread

Inanna's bounty

- 25mm yellow quartz donut
- 14mm red magma crystal round rings
- 14mm tabac crystal square rings
- 8mm topaz bicones
- 6mm topaz bicones
- 4mm Bordeaux crystal pearls
- 4mm topaz bicones
- Lemon celsian bricks
- Halo sandalwood bricks
- Honey-lined berry beads
- 3mm peridot bicones
- 3mm light peach crystal pearls
- 3mm gold crystal pearls
- 3mm copper crystal pearls
- 3mm Bordeaux crystal pearls
- Gold-lined AB 11ºs
- Garnet-lined ruby 11ºs
- Semi-matte peach-lined topaz 11ºs
- Gold-lined peridot AB 11ºs
- Silver-lined light olivine 11ºs
- Light daffodil 15ºs
- Transparent chartreuse AB 15ºs
- Cranberry-lined topaz 15ºs
- Dark peach-lined crystal AB 15ºs
- Butter yellow ceylon 15ºs

b

c

8. String a heishi, an 8mm bicone, a heishi, a 4mm pearl, a 3mm spacer, a 3mm pearl, an 11º, a gold-lined crystal AB 15º seed bead, and a Temple element as shown (**photo b**).

9. String a 15º, an 11º, a 3mm pearl, a 3mm spacer, a 4mm pearl, a heishi, an 8mm bicone, a heishi, a 4mm pearl, a 3mm spacer, a 3mm pearl, an 11º and a 15º.

10. String through a brick in the Trefoil Connector, pick up fifteen 15ºs, and string through the last brick in the Trefoil Connector (**photo c**).

11. String a 15º, an 11º, a 3mm pearl, a 3mm spacer, a 4mm pearl, a heishi, an 8mm bicone, a heishi, a 4mm pearl, a 3mm spacer, a 3mm pearl, an 11º, and a 15º.

12. String a Temple, a 15º, an 11º, a 3mm pearl, a 3mm spacer, a 4mm pearl, a heishi, an 8mm bicone, a heishi, a 4mm pearl,

a 3mm spacer, a 3mm pearl, an 11º, a Turban, two 11ºs, a 3mm pearl, and a 3mm spacer.

13. String a 4mm pearl, a heishi, an 8mm bicone, a heishi, a 4mm pearl, a 3mm spacer, a 6mm bicone, and a 3mm spacer. Repeat this step twice.

14. String three 3mm pearls, a 3mm spacer, a 4mm bicone, a 3mm spacer, three 3mm pearls, and a crimp bead.

15. Crimp both ends of the beading wire. Remember to slip the clasps into the wire guardians before crimping them. However, if you forget, you can always connect the clasp with a couple of oval jump rings.

Far Horizons
necklace

The graduated components featured in this necklace draw the eye to your masterpiece of a Sunburst pendant, graced with the swag embellishment. The instructions make a necklace about 19" long.

Rosy haze colorway

materials

tumbling blocks (2)
- **14** gold-marbled green emerald two-hole tiles
- **16** 4mm emerald bicones
- **28** 4mm dark lapis crystal pearls
- **1.25g** opaque cobalt luster 11º seed beads
- **1.25g** lime-lined crystal AB 15º seed beads

coffee bean links (2)
- **16** ultramarine halo two-hole lentils
- **8** crystal AB berry beads
- **.5g** opaque cobalt luster 11ºs
- **.5g** silver-lined emerald 15ºs

jewel-encased rings (2)
- **12** gold-marbled green emerald two-hole tiles
- **12** 4mm emerald bicones
- **24** 3mm dark lapis crystal pearls
- **.5g** opaque cobalt luster 11ºs
- **.5g** lime-lined crystal AB 15ºs

sunburst swag (1) with herringbone bar connectors
- **14mm** peridot rivoli
- **16** iris-lustered cobalt two-hole daggers
- **6** 4mm emerald bicones
- **4** 3mm dark lapis crystal pearls
- **.25g** opaque cobalt luster 11ºs
- **.75g** silver-lined emerald 15ºs (color F)
- **.75g** lime-lined crystal AB 15ºs (color G)

other materials
- **8** 4mm soldered jump rings
- **2** 6x5mm oval jump rings
- Sun-themed toggle clasp
- Size D nylon thread

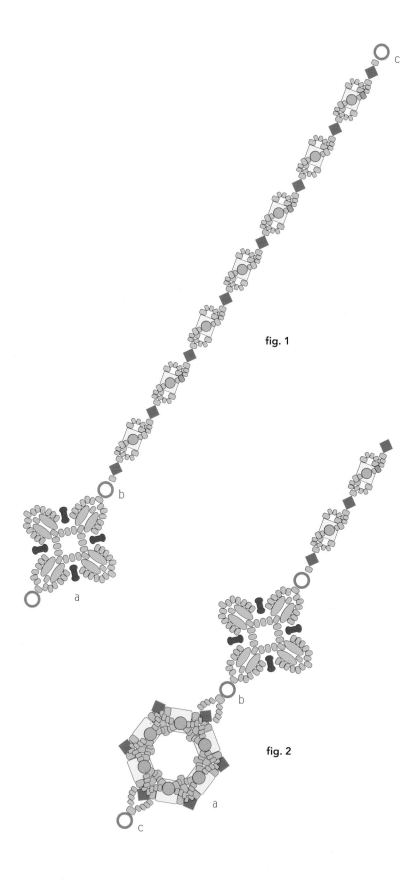

fig. 1

fig. 2

fig. 3

Rosy haze

- 14mm opaque dark olive button bead
- Pink/topaz luster two-hole tiles
- Luster transparent topaz/pink halo two-hole lentils
- Luster pink crystal two-hole daggers
- Gray rainbow luster berry beads
- 4mm dark green crystal pearls
- 4mm garnet AB bicones
- 3mm dark green crystal pearls
- 3mm powder green crystal pearls
- Brown iris 11ºs
- Green iris 11ºs
- Gold-lined rainbow crystal 11ºs
- Purple iris 15ºs
- Green iris 15ºs

tools
- Size 12 and 13 needles
- Silicon thread conditioner
- Thread snips

1. Make two Coffee Bean Links, p. 30. Make them with two jump rings opposite each other **(fig. 1, a)**.

2. Make a Tumbling Blocks strap, p. 52, with seven tiles. Connect one end to a jump ring on a Coffee Bean Link **(b)**. Attach a new soldered jump ring to the other end of the strap **(c)**. Make a second strap like the first, connecting it to the other Coffee Bean Link.

3. Make a Jewel-Encased Ring, p. 10 **(fig, 2, a)**. Connect it to the free ring on a Coffee Bean Link **(b)**. Add a second jump ring across

from the first one **(c)**. Make a second Jewel-Encased Ring and connect it to the free Coffee Bean Link. Add a second jump ring across from the first.

4. Make a Sunburst Swag, p. 43. Add a thread as explained on p. 45. Add two Herringbone Bar Connectors, p. 46. Connect one bar to a free jump ring on a Jewel-Encased Ring. Connect the second bar to the other Jewel-Encased Ring's free jump ring **(fig. 3)**.

5. Use oval jump rings to connect the clasp.

Autumn fairy colorway

Lewis Carroll was a curious man. Since one of his poems explains the best time for seeing fairies, it seems appropriate that a necklace featuring the Flower Fairy element be named in his honor.

Lewis Carroll's Garden *necklace*

Ideally, you want 17 or 19 links in your chain. Both samples have 17 links. Be sure to use round links. Oval ones end up looking strange in the center.

1. Make a Flower Fairy, p. 34. Start the second fairy by tying a lark's head knot to the ring at the top of the first fairy (otherwise, there is nothing different about the second fairy). Start the third fairy the same way as the second. Weave in the threads as explained in option B of step 12 in the Flower Fairy instructions. Make two fairy chains for each necklace.

2. Make the straps: Refer to Titania's Strap, p. 53. Each strap in this necklace has 46 rows of beads. Sew jump rings on only one end of each strap as in step 6. Attach the fairy to the end with no jump ring by picking up one 11º seed bead, sewing through the 11º at the center top of the fairy, picking up another 11º, and sewing up through a few beads in one column of the strap and back down through the same number (fig. 1, p. 108). Sew through the 11ºs connecting the fairy and the strap a few more times to strengthen the connection. Sew up and down through a different number of beads in the strap each time so you don't build up a crossbar of thread in any one place. Weave the tail in and secure it with a couple of slip knots. Trim the excess thread.

Autumn fairy colorway: Refer to the instructions for the Diamond Deluxe Strap, p. 55. Each Diamond Deluxe Strap has nine sections. Follow the instructions as they are given for the first eight sections. When you start the ninth section, things change at step 4. Instead of picking up a second 11º, sew through the 11º at the center top of the last Flower Fairy in a chain (fig. 2, p. 108). Return to the strap instructions and complete the ninth section as usual. When the ninth section is complete, reinforce the connection between the strap and the Flower Fairies. If possible, try to sew through the 11ºs on the Flower

materials

Titania's strap (2)
- **30** blue iris two-hole lentils
- **2.5g** silver-lined Capri blue AB 8º seed beads
- **.25g** mint green Ceylon 11º seed beads
- **.5g** blue turquoise 15º seed beads (color A)
- **.5g** silver-lined blue zircon 15ºs (color B)

flower fairies (6)
- **18** jet peacock two-hole daggers
- **12** 8/7 milky peridot petals
- **18** blue iris two-hole lentils
- **1g** mint green Ceylon 11ºs
- **.75** silver-lined light emerald 15ºs

coffee bean links (2)
- **16** blue iris two-hole lentils
- **8** aqua green lined berry beads
- **.5g** mint green Ceylon 11ºs
- **.5g** opaque blue turquoise 15ºs

jewel-encased ring (1)
- **6** blue iris tiles
- **6** 4mm light turquoise bicones
- **12** 3mm turquoise crystal pearls
- **1g** mint green Ceylon 11ºs
- **.75g** silver-lined blue zircon 15ºs

radiant clasp (1)
- **10** blue iris SuperDuos
- **2** 4mm heishi
- **2** 3mm turquoise 3mm pearls
- **.75g** mint green 11ºs
- **.25g** blue turquoise 15ºs
- **2** silver-lined blue zircon 15ºs

other materials
- **2"** rolo chain, 4mm links
- **5** 20-gauge small oval jump rings
- **11** 4mm soldered jump rings
- Size D nylon thread

Autumn fairy

- Jet bronze picasso two-hole daggers
- Bronze iris two-hole lentils
- Bronze iris tiles
- 8/7 halo linen petals
- Honey-lined berry beads
- 4mm jet nut 2x bicones
- 3mm rose gold crystal pearls
- Silver-lined peach smoke 6⁰s
- Brown iris 8⁰s
- Matte topaz 11⁰s
- Silver-lined root beer AB 11⁰s
- Silver-lined light gold 15⁰s

tools
- Size 10 and 12 needles
- Silicon thread conditioner
- Thread snips
- Chainnose pliers
- Flush or wire cutters

Fairy's back at least once so the center top 11⁰ doesn't have to take the strain of the connection. Continue weaving the center 11⁰s into the strap. Weave the tail into the strap, securing it with a couple of slip knots. Trim the excess thread. Sew a jump ring to the other end of each strap as in step 6.

3. Make two Coffee Bean Links, p. 30 (these only have one soldered jump ring).

4. Make one Jewel-Encased Ring, p. 10. Only sew on one jump ring.

5. Add the clasp: Use two oval jump rings to connect the clasp to the straps. Make a Radiant Clasp, p. 50. Sew the clasp directly to the jump rings at the ends of the straps.

6. Find the center link of your chain (make sure you have an odd number of links). Connect the Jewel-Encased Ring to the center link with an oval jump ring. Use two more oval jump rings to connect the Coffee Bean Links to the second-to-last links on either end of the chain. Make sure the chain hasn't twisted—the Jewel-Encased Ring and Coffee Bean Links must hang from the same side of the chain. Use the last two oval jump rings to connect the ends of the chain to the jump rings at the bottoms of the Flower Fairy chains.

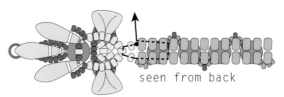

seen from back

fig. 1

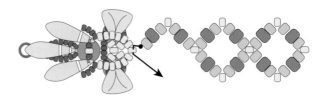

fig. 2

Rose Window
necklace

This necklace shows off your bead-weaving skills with a delicate look. The main colorway shows you how to adjust the count for a cabochon that is proportioned differently than a rivoli. The second variation uses both kinds of crystals and two color schemes to highlight the different crystals.

Evening lagoon colorway

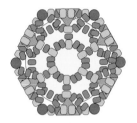

fig. 1

fig. 2

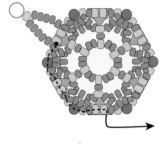

fig. 3

Main colorway

1. Make three Lattice Bezels, p. 22. If you are using a glass cabochon: In step 6, pick up two 15⁰s instead of one, and then sew through the next 11⁰ **(fig. 1)**. Bundle the thread as you finish the first two. After you finish the third lattice, work your needle and thread through two 11⁰s on the outside of a triangle.

Use crystal rivolis instead of glass cabochons, if desired.

2. Pick up four 15⁰s and an 11⁰, and sew through a soldered jump ring and back through the 11⁰ and 15⁰s. Continue through two 11⁰s **(fig. 2)**. Pick up four 15⁰s and sew through an 11⁰ and the soldered jump ring. Sew back through the 11⁰ and the four 15⁰s. Sew through all the beads connecting the jump ring again. Sew the thread in, securing it with a couple of slip knots. Avoid the two 11⁰s directly opposite the ones connected to the jump ring.

3. Unbundle the thread on the second Lattice Bezel. Thread a

needle and repeat step 2.

4. To make the center lattice, repeat step 3 with the third Lattice Bezel. This time, pick up five 15⁰s instead of four. Tighten the tension by sewing through the two 11⁰s on the outside of the triangle. Continue sewing through a 15⁰, an 11⁰, a pearl, an 11⁰, a 15⁰, two 11⁰s, 15⁰, an 11⁰, a pearl, an 11⁰, a 15⁰, and two 11⁰s **(fig. 3)**. This completes the center lattice.

5. *Pick up a 15⁰, and sew through the two 11⁰s opposite the jump ring on one of the first two lattices. Pick up a 15⁰, and sew through the two 11⁰s on the center lattice **(fig. 4)**. Sew through these 11⁰s and 15⁰s a few more times to strengthen the connection. End by sewing through the two 11⁰s on the center lattice.* Continue sewing through a 15⁰, an 11⁰, a pearl, an 11⁰, a 15⁰, two 11⁰s, 15⁰, an 11⁰, a pearl, an 11⁰, a 15⁰, and two 11⁰s. Repeat the section between the *. Weave the thread in, securing it with a couple of slip knots. Trim the excess thread.

6. On a decorative headpin, string a drop (point down), a bead cap, a bicone, and a spacer. Make a wrapped loop to connect the dangle to the center jump ring.

7. Cut the chain in two equal pieces. Use oval jump rings to connect one end of each chain to the side jump rings. Use the remaining two jump rings to connect the clasp to the ends.

Evening lagoon colorway

1. Separate the starred materials from the unstarred materials.

2. Using the unstarred set of materials, make a Latice Bezel. End by working your needle through two 11⁰s on the outside of a triangle. Pick up four 15⁰s and an 11⁰. Sew through a soldered jump ring and back through the 11⁰ and 15⁰s. Continue through two 11⁰s **(fig. 4)**. Pick up four 15⁰s and sew through an 11⁰ and the soldered jump ring. Sew back through the 11⁰ and the four 15⁰s. Sew through

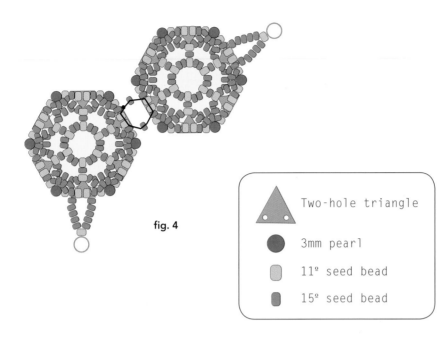

fig. 4

Two-hole triangle

3mm pearl

11º seed bead

15º seed bead

materials
- **3** 15mm faceted glass cabochons
- 9x6 tanzanite AB crystal drop
- Light olivine 4mm bicone
- **18** two-hole purple suede triangles
- **18** 3mm lavender crystal pearls
- **2** 2.5mm spacers
- .75g silver-lined chartreuse 11º seed beads
- .75 silver-lined light amethyst 15º seed beads
- 1' textured heart chain
- 7mm bead cap
- 2" decorative headpin
- **2** 6mm twisted jump rings
- **2** 6x4 oval jump rings
- **3** 3–4mm soldered jump rings
- Heart lobster claw clasp
- Heart end ring
- Size D nylon thread

Evening lagoon

- **2** 14mm emerald rivolis
- 14mm Bermuda blue crystal ring*
- 15x8 light emerald glass drop
- metallic blue 4mm bicone
- **18** turquoise suede two-hole triangles
- **12** 3mm turquoise crystal pearls
- **6** 3mm petrol crystal pearls*
- 2.5mm spacer
- 1g light sapphire/metallic teal-lined 11ºs
- .75g blue iris 11ºs*
- 1g blue-green transparent 15ºs
- .5g silver-lined light green 15ºs*
- 1' bar chain
- 8mm bead cap
- 2" decorative headpin
- **4** 6x4 oval jump rings
- **3** 3–4mm soldered jump rings
- Lobster-claw clasp
- Soldered jump ring

tools
- Size 12 needles
- Silicon thread conditioner
- Thread snips

all the beads connecting the jump ring again to reinforce them and tighten the tension. Sew the thread in, securing it with a couple of slip knots. Avoid the two 11ºs directly opposite the ones connected to the jump ring.

3. Repeat step 2 to make a second Lattice Bezel with a jump ring.

4. Using the starred set of materials, make one Lattice Bezel. This will be your center lattice. End by working your needle and thread through two 11ºs on the outside of a triangle. Pick up five 15ºs and an 11º. Sew through a soldered jump ring and back through the 11º and 15ºs. Continue through two 11ºs. Pick up five 15ºs and sew through an 11º and the soldered jump ring. Sew back through the 11º and the 15ºs. Sew through all the beads connecting the jump ring again to reinforce them and tighten the tension. Finish tightening the tension by sewing through the two 11ºs on the outside of the triangle. *Continue sewing through a 15º, an

11º, a pearl, an 11º, a 15º, two 11ºs, 15º, an 11º, a pearl, an 11º, a 15º, and two 11ºs. Pick up a 15º. Sew through the two 11ºs opposite the jump ring on one of the first two lattices. Pick up a 15º. Sew through the two 11ºs on the center lattice **(fig. 4)**. Sew through these 11ºs and 15ºs a few more times to strengthen and tighten the connection between the two lattices. End by sewing through the two 11ºs on the center lattice.* Repeat the section between the *. Weave the thread in, securing it with a couple of slip knots. Trim the excess thread.

5. On the headpin, string the drop, point down; the bead cap, a spacer, a bicone, and a spacer. Use a wrapped loop to connect the dangle to the center jump ring.

6. Cut the chain in two equal pieces. Using the twisted jump rings, connect one end of each chain to the side jump rings. Use the oval jump rings to connect the clasp to the ends.

gallery

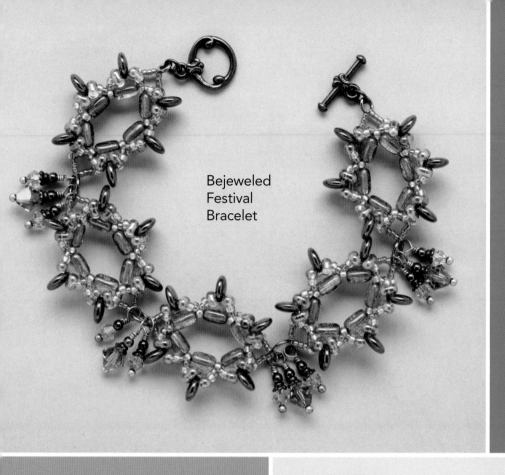

Bejeweled
Festival
Bracelet

Origami/
Right Angle Tango
Earrings

Pacifica Variation:
Mountain Heather

Lewis Carroll
Variation

Titania's Wrap Bracelet

Simple Sunburst

Dark Light

Delicate Dangle
Pendant

Double Tumblers
Bracelet

Coffee Bean
Dangles Earrings

basics

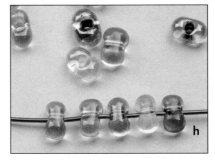

Beads

The element and projects in this book feature a variety of shaped two-hole and one-hole glass beads. All the samples in this book were made with Czech two-hole beads. I do not recommend that you use Japanese versions, because the holes are spaced differently and the beads with similar names to Czech versions are shaped a bit differently. Also, not all of the two-hole shapes available in the Czech varieties are available from Japanese manufacturers. The Czech glass beads are daggers **(a)**, tiles **(b)**, bricks **(c)**, two-hole lentils **(d)**, one-hole lentils **(e)**, two-hole triangles **(f)**,

and SuperDuos **(g)**. The other shaped bead is sometimes called "berry," "peanut," or "farfelle" **(h)**. I have called this shape "berry" throughout the book. You'll also see seed beads and crystals of various sizes included in the materials sections of everything. Use Japanese seed beads—these are readily available in a seemingly limitless variety of finishes and colors and are more consistent in size than Czech seed beads.

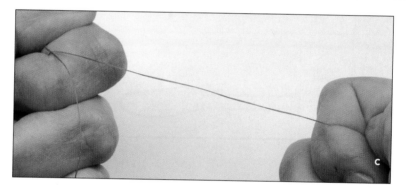

Needles, Thread, and Conditioner

Use long, high-quality beading needles. The eyes have cleaner holes and the tips are less likely to have burrs. Longer needles make it easier to pick up seed beads—use the needle instead of your fingers to pick them up **(a)**. Most of the time, you will be instructed to use either a size 10 or 12 needle. The higher the number, the smaller the needle (and the more difficult it is to thread). Always keep size 13 needles on hand as well. Use the 13s only if a bead is too tight to allow a 12 to pass through. Also, consider the 13s a one-use needle. Often, the eye collapses so much when one of these needles is pulled through a snug bead that it cannot be threaded again. If you have beads that seem to have holes that run small, test them with a size 10 needle and set aside or discard any that will not allow a size 10 needle to go through them.

There are many thread options out there, including nylon thread and bonded or braided beading thread. **(b)** People tend to have a favorite, and I prefer nylon threads in bobbins or cones to the braided or bonded varieties that come on spools. All of the samples in this book were made with C-lon size D thread. Nylon threads have a much greater variety of color choices. Some people don't wax the nylon threads, but I find it makes beadweaving easier. Use a silicon thread conditioner, not wax, to condition your thread (wax can gunk up the holes of a 15° seed bead and will stain matte finishes). Stretch and condition the thread before threading on a needle: First, cut the specified length. Hold the thread with your hands approximately a foot apart and gently pull the thread to stretch it **(c)**. Work your way from one end to the other. The curl will come out of the thread as you stretch it.

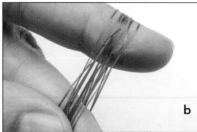

Bundling Thread

This is a handy technique for saving thread if you're not sure yet how you're going to finish off a component or include it in a piece of jewelry. First, prepare a piece of tape by folding over the ends **(a)**. Next, wrap the thread around a couple of your fingers **(b)**. Now, twist the thread into a figure 8 **(c)**. Fold the tape around the thread where it crosses itself **(d)**.

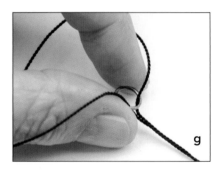

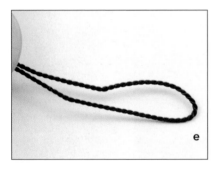

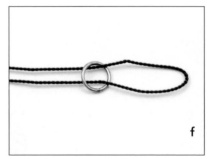

Tying a Lark's Head Knot

This is a useful knot because it is small and tidy. Fold the thread in half **(e)**. Pass the fold through a soldered jump ring **(f)**. Put your thumb and forefinger through the loop, and pull the jump ring through the loop to tighten the knot **(g)**.

Threading a Needle

Beading needles have narrow eyes. Often, the braided and bonded threads need to be flattened with a pair of chainnose pliers before you can thread them. Regular nylon threads can be flattened between your fingers. Once flattened, hold the thread between your thumb and forefinger so that you can just barely see the thread. Hold the needle's eye just above the thread and roll the thread up through the eye. This can take practice.

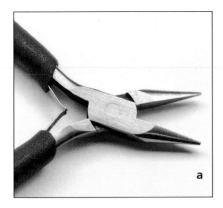
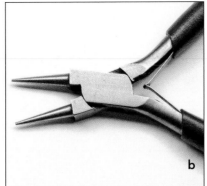

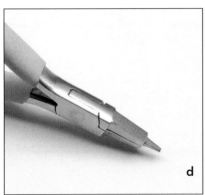

Tools

Some of the projects in this book require tools such as chainnose pliers **(a)**, roundnose pliers **(b)**, flush cutters **(c)**, 1mm roundnose pliers (which I like to call my 'cheater tool') **(d)**, crimping pliers **(e)**, and macro crimpers **(f)**. There is no one tool that will do it all, so don't be tempted by one of those all-in-one tools. The purpose of each tool will be explained in relevant sections.

Setting Up a Mat

If you are new to beadweaving or are using unfamiliar shapes or sizes, it is very helpful to set up your work surface with labels for the different beads. It's also a good way to keep from getting mixed up when you use two colors of the same size bead. Use clear tape and write the name of the bead (or its size or size and symbol) on the tape. I like to put the label above my bead piles; some people put them below.

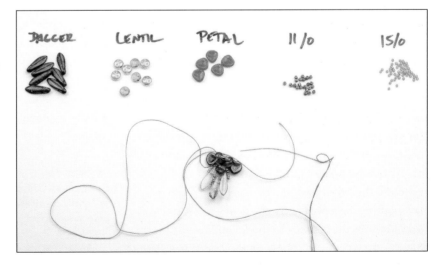

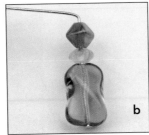
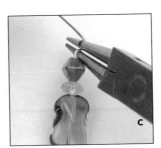
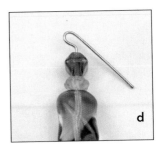

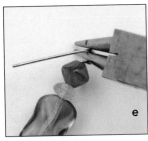

Making a Perfect Wrapped Loop

You have to practice, practice, practice wrapped loops to learn them. It requires muscle memory to be able to do them smoothly and easily. Once you've gotten the technique down, you'll be able to do it without thinking about each micro-step.

First, stack your beads on a headpin as directed. Next, hold the headpin with the 1mm pliers butted up next to the beads—the pliers must touch the beads. Bend the wire (do not bend the tool) against the top-side of the plier jaws at a 90-degree (right) angle (a). Set aside the 1mm pliers and note that there is a small space between the corner and the beads (b). Make a mark with a permanent marker on the roundnose pliers approximately ¼" from the tips. Using the mark as a guide, place the bent headpin in the pliers so that the beads hang down and the bend end sticks straight out from the jaws like a cigar. Going *up* and *over* the pliers, wrap the wire around only the upper jaw of the pliers (c). Look carefully at the wire in relationship to the pliers—notice the gap between the beads and the bend as well as how the loop sticks out to the side (d). Switch the position of the partial loop so that it is around the lower jaw (e). You can do this either by turning the pliers over or by physically moving the headpin from the top jaw to the lower jaw. Make sure that the partial loop is snugly on the pliers' jaw. Fix the image of a snowman in your mind: you want to end up with a roundish circle centered over the beads. The straight bit of wire is like a scarf in a stiff breeze. This

is the hard part: keep the wire on the pliers and alternate between pushing the corner against the pliers and sweeping the straight end across the corner.

You want the wire to cross exactly over the corner, so whatever you do, do not straighten out the corner (f). Set aside the roundnose pliers. Hold the circle flat in a pair of chainnose pliers. Use your left hand to hold the chainnose pliers if you are right-handed and in your right hand if you are left-handed. Hold the end of the straight wire with the roundnose pliers in your dominant hand. Starting in the corner, wrap the wire around the bit between the corner and the beads (g). Place each wrap next to the one before, with no space showing between them. Stop wrapping when you meet the beads. Trim the excess wire with your flush cutters—always put the flat side of the cutter against the piece of jewelry (h). Very little wire should stick out. If you have as much as ⅛", get in there and trim again.

SAFETY TIP: **Cover the wire when you are trimming the excess. These small bits can fly surprisingly far and are very dangerous if they hit you in the eye. You can also wear safety goggles.**

There probably is a sharp nubbin sticking out no matter how closely you trimmed. Using chainnose pliers, gently guide this sharp tip into place next to the beads.

 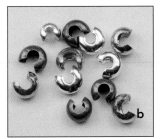 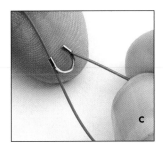 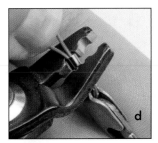

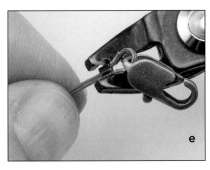 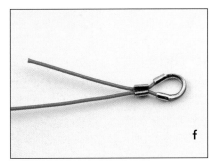 

Crimping

To successfully and professionally crimp your jewelry, you will need wire guardians or thimbles (a) and crimp covers (b). I recommend that you only use 2x2mm crimp tubes for the projects in this book. Do not use round crimp beads because they are not as durable. Before you start, take a look at your crimping tool and notice the two sets of notches. The outside one is smooth and sort almond-shaped when seen from the side. The other notch looks like a pair of cartoon lips. Also, look at the difference between the sizes of the notches between the regular crimp tool and the macro crimper. Use only the regular crimp tool to crimp the 2x2 crimp tubes used in these projects.

String the beads as directed on beading wire—the last bead on the wire will be a crimp tube. Pass the wire through a wire guardian (c). Hook part of the clasp into the guardian, and then pass the wire back through the crimp tube. Leaving a small space between the crimp tube and the guardian, hold the crimp tube in the pair of lips notch (d). Squeeze hard. Remove the crimped tube and look for the groove that runs along it. Place the tube in the almond notch so that you can see the groove (e). Squeeze again. Put some backbone into it: A properly crimped tube will look like someone thin-lipping you (f). Trim the excess bit of beading wire with a pair of flush cutters— scissors will not work.

Hold the crimp cover in the almond notch of the macro crimper so you can see the opening of the cover and set the crimp tube inside—make sure the tube is complete seated inside the cover (g). Sometimes you have to open the covers a little more with an awl or the tip of your roundnose pliers. Gently squeeze the pliers to close the cover. If necessary, adjust the way the pliers hold the cover and squeeze a little more.

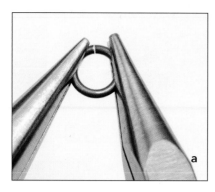

Opening and Closing Jump Rings

You will find that 4mm soldered jump rings are frequently referenced in these projects. (Don't try to cheat and use non-soldered jump rings; beading wire is thin, and it will find a way to slip through any small cracks, no matter how well you close a jump ring.) Fortunately, soldered jump rings are available in any finish you could want: silver, gold, plated, solid brass, copper and gun metal. The other frequently used jump ring is an oval jump ring. I prefer to use these for connections because they are slightly more secure.

I also recommend using nothing finer than 20-gauge. Opening and closing round or oval jump rings is easier if you have two pairs of chainnose pliers, but you can use one chain and one roundnose. Hold the jump ring on either side of the cut (a). Twist one hand toward you and one hand away (b). Put whatever is supposed to go inside the ring inside it and twist back to center. Go slightly past center, and then align the two ends of the ring with each other. Going slightly past center and then back makes the jump ring stronger.

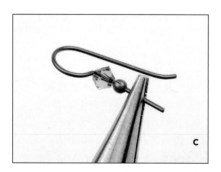

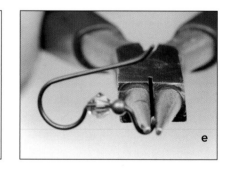

Completing Ear Wires

Opening the loop at the bottom of the ear wire is similar to opening a jump ring, although one pair of pliers usually does the trick. You may not know about ear wire blanks—these are a simple way to customize ear wires to complement your designs. Blanks are French hooks that have no bottom loop. First, string a 3–4mm accent ead that complements your design, and then string a round spacer bead about 1–2mm wide (this is especially important if you choose a crystal bicone for your accent bead).

If you can only fit a 3mm or 4mm bead on the wire, use a metal bead. Leaving a small gap, hold the remainder of the wire with a pair of chainnose pliers (c). Bend the wire at a right angle. Using a pair of roundnose pliers, hold the end of the wire in the roundnose pliers so that you can just barely feel the tip (d). Roll the roundnose over so that the end of the wire meets the right-angle corner (e).

Using Epoxy Clay

You will see that a few projects include an optional finishing touch using epoxy clay. There are a few different kinds of this two-part clay available for the jewelry/craft markets and they are all easy to use. Clean your hands after you have mixed the clay and before touching the crystal embellishments. Protect your work surface with a sheet of parchment paper. Thoroughly mix equal parts of A and B of the clay. Each part is half what you need to barely fill your cavity. If you didn't mix enough, you can always mix a

little more. Shape the mixed clay into a very thick pancake. Lightly press the clay in place as directed in the instructions—note that there is a depression in the center of the clay (a). Pick up your crystal with a clean hand and center it on the clay. Press the crystal in place with a pencil eraser (b). Use an inexpensive craft paintbrush to dust the clay with mica powder (c). Allow the clay to cure according to the manufacturer's instructions. Brush off any stray mica powder.

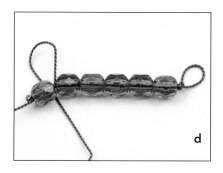

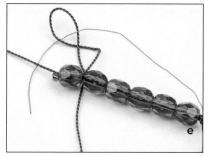

Tying a Slip Knot

Try to tie at least one slip knot before you trim the thread. The knot helps anchor the thread. Pull the thread completely through a bead and wrap the thread in a small loose circle around the thread in the beadwork (d). Use the needle to twist the circle into a figure 8 (e). Pull the needle through the figure 8 and

carefully tighten the knot so that it falls between the last bead you passed through and the next bead (f). Sew through a few beads and tie another knot, if possible. Otherwise, trim the thread. Always sew through a few beads after tying a knot and before trimming the excess thread.

Resources

Chances are, if you're reading this book, that you already know your way around online. As a bead store owner, I encourage you to check with your local bead store first and see what they have. Everything I've used in the projects is readily available, and it's very likely that, like Dorothy, "you'll find what you need in your own back yard."

Acknowledgments

First, I must thank Nedda Rovelli, without whom Ubeadquitous never would have happened. She deserves special appreciation for her work on the process shots.

Special thanks are also due Erica Swanson, my editor at Kalmbach, who fished the original query letter out of the pile and worked liked a demon to make this book happen. Thanks also to Bill Zuback for advice and assistance with photography and Kellie Jaeger for teaching me some fine points about using Illustrator, and for their work on the final photography and illustrations. Many thanks to Lisa Bergman for her art direction on the final design of this book.

Thanks also to Su Lin Mangan, Jennifer Garcia, Juanita Langley, Brenda Balding, Gretchen Olt, Marilyn Bishop, and other dedicated beaders for their loyalty over the years. Grateful thanks to Phyllis Nash-Haley, Barbara Derringer, Terry Schmidt, and Ginny Ward for their assistance while I was writing this book.

About the Author

Although I only hazily remember it, my grandmother taught me to make beaded ropes like ones she wore in her flapper days. When I was twelve, my parents gave me a loom and my friends and I spent hours making rings with secret messages in them on the loom. Many years later, I discovered hand-weaving and spoiled all my friends and family after that with gifts of hand-woven beaded jewelry on every conceivable occasion. After being downsized from a job as a college bookstore manager, I threw caution to the wind and decided to open a bead store. Since then, I've had a couple of patterns published in beading magazines and was a Starman Trendsetter in 2013.

I'd love to see what you do, and so would other people. As a convenient forum, I've started a Facebook page called *Component Stitching*; please feel free to upload a photo of your design or a project from the book done in colors you chose.

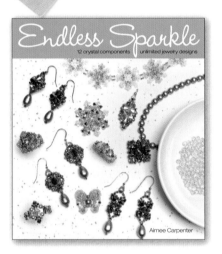
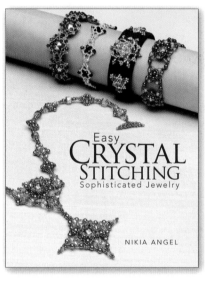